GLUTEN FREE BAKING

Michael McCamley

GLUTEN FREE BAKING

Just as delicious—just as easy

This edition published by Parragon Books Ltd in 2014
LOVE FOOD is an imprint of Parragon Books Ltd

Parragon Inc.
440 Park Avenue South, 13th Floor
New York, NY 10016

www.parragon.com/lovefood

ISBN: 978-1-4723-7701-2

Printed in China

Recipes by Michael McCamley
Photography by Noel Murphy
Home Economy by Jane Lawrie
Design by Lexi L'Esteve

"For my Mother Annie (1929–1989), who inspired me to achieve."

Notes for the Reader
This book uses standard kitchen measuring spoons and cups. All spoon and cup measurements are level
unless otherwise indicated. Unless otherwise stated, milk is assumed to be whole, butter is assumed to
be salted, eggs are large, individual vegetables are medium, and pepper is freshly ground black pepper.
Unless otherwise stated, all root vegetables should be washed and peeled before using.

Garnishes and serving suggestions are all optional and not necessarily included in the recipe ingredients
or method.

The times given are only an approximate guide. Preparation times differ according to the techniques
used by different people and the cooking times may also vary from those given. Optional ingredients,
variations, or serving suggestions have not been included in the calculations.

Recipes using raw or very lightly cooked eggs should be avoided by infants, the elderly, pregnant
women, and people with weakened immune systems. Pregnant and breast-feeding women are advised
to avoid eating peanuts and peanut products. People with nut allergies should be aware that some of
the prepared ingredients used in the recipes in this book may contain nuts. Always check the packaging
before use.

Contents

Introduction

What is Gluten?

Gluten is a mixture of two proteins, gliadin and glutenin, that is found in wheat, rye, and barley and ingredients derived from these cereals. When the grain is milled, it is the gluten that gives the flour its elasticity. The majority of people can eat gluten without any implications or long term adverse effects; however, it can cause mild to severe problems for individuals with celiac disease or gluten intolerance. The difference between celiac disease and gluten intolerance/sensitivity can be confusing. However, one thing is certain: once a diagnosis has been made, a gluten-free diet is the universal treatment for both conditions.

Celiac Disease

pronounced "see-lee-ack" celiac disease is commonly regarded as a food allergy or intolerance, however, it is actually an autoimmune disease caused by eating gluten. People with celiac disease make antibodies against gluten, so even a small amount can trigger an immune reaction in people with the condition. Eating gluten damages the lining of the small intestine, and other parts of the body may be affected in the long term. Small fingerlike projections called villi line the small intestine, and they play a significant role in food digestion. When the villi are damaged and inflamed, they are unable to absorb food properly, so that the food and nutrients are not properly digested, which often causes diarrhea, malnutrition, and other health problems. If celiac disease is left undiagnosed or if a gluten-free diet is not adhered to following a diagnosis, those with the disease have an increased risk of developing other associated diseases. These include osteoporosis, lymphoma, and other autoimmune diseases, such as type 1 diabetes, thyroid disease, rheumatoid arthritis, inflammatory bowel disease, Sjögren's syndrome, and lupus.

Who Can Get Celiac Disease?

The cause of celiac disease is unknown; however, it is thought to be a combination of genetic and environmental factors. If a close family member—

for example, a brother, sister, parent, or child—has been diagnosed, then there is a one-in-ten chance of having celiac disease. Although approximately 1 in 100 people are thought to have celiac disease, many are undiagnosed or misdiagnosed as having other types of digestive conditions. Research has shown that the average length of time it takes for a confirmed diagnosis is approximately 13 years. Celiac disease can develop at any age and, for many years, it was believed to be a childhood disease that you could grow out of; it is most frequently diagnosed, however, between the ages of 40 to 60 years. Contrary to common belief, celiac disease affects all ethnic groups and is found in Europe and North America, as well as in South America, Southern Asia, North Africa, and the Middle East. It is most commonly found in countries where wheat plays a large part in the everyday diet.

Symptoms

There are many indicators for celiac disease, but because people have a unique mixture of symptoms, it is often difficult to pinpoint celiac disease as the cause. Many of the symptoms mimic or are similar to other diseases, such as irritable bowel syndrome, so it can take years to obtain an accurate diagnosis. The symptoms can vary from person to person and can include one or a combination of the following:

- recurrent gastrointestinal symptoms, such as nausea, vomiting, and diarrhea
- excessive flatulence, and/or constipation
- persistent stomach pain, cramping, or bloating
- iron, vitamin B_{12} or folic acid deficiency
- tiredness
- headaches
- weight loss (but not in all cases)
- canker sores
- hair loss (alopecia)
- skin rash (dermatitis herpetiformis, DH)
- tooth enamel problems
- osteoporosis
- depression and anxiety
- infertility or repeated miscarriages
- joint and/or bone pain
- neurological problems, such as ataxia and neuropathy.

Symptoms in babies and young children can also include:

- a bloated stomach
- muscle wasting in the arms and legs
- irritability
- failure to gain or lose weight.

Diagnosis

The first step to diagnosis is discussing the symptoms with a physician. If your physician suspects you have celiac disease, he or she will perform a careful physical examination and will discuss your medical history with you. A blood test should then be taken in order to detect the presence of antibodies that are produced in response to digested gluten. Your doctor may arrange additional tests to detect nutritional deficiencies, such as a blood test to detect iron levels, because anemia can often occur with celiac disease. A stool sample may be tested to detect fat in the stool, because celiac disease prevents fat from being absorbed from food. The doctor should then refer you to a gastroenterologist for a biopsy of the digestive tract to test the villi of the small intestine for damage. In a biopsy, the doctor inserts an endoscope (a thin, hollow tube) through your mouth and into the small intestine, and takes a sample of the small intestine with an instrument to examine under a microscope. This is the best way to confirm if you have celiac disease. More recently, home testing kits for celiac disease have become available over the counter and online, but these are not always reliable and any results should be discussed and confirmed by your physician.

Treatment

Celiac disease cannot be cured, so, if a positive diagnosis is confirmed, the only treatment to enable repair of the small intestine and to alleviate the symptoms is to embark on a completely gluten-free diet. This requires considerable support and information. After diagnosis a referral to a Registered Dietician (RD) should be made, where advice for following a completely gluten-free diet will be given. If tests show that nutrient levels are low,

vitamins and minerals may be recommended. Following a strict gluten-free diet will also reduce the risk of osteoporosis, cancer, and associated autoimmune diseases.

False Negative Tests

Many people have negative results to the tests for celiac disease, however, they still have the same symptoms whenever gluten is digested. In this case, they may have had false negative tests. In order to be sure that they do not have false negative tests for celiac disease, they need to continue to eat gluten until the tests have been completed. Abstaining from foods containing gluten will prevent the immune system from producing the antibodies needed for detection in the blood test. Abstaining from gluten prior to the biopsy may also cause the villi in the small intestine to show signs of repair, making it difficult for the gastroenterologist to make a conclusive diagnosis of celiac disease.

Nonceliac Gluten Intolerance

If, however, genuine negative test results for celiac disease are received and symptoms are still being experienced, a person may instead have nonceliac gluten intolerance. Because it shares many of the characteristics of celiac disease, such as bowel problems, tiredness, and depression, it is possible that a misdiagnosis can be made. Nonceliac gluten intolerance is thought to affect approximately 15 percent of the world's population, the majority of whom are still undiagnosed or misdiagnosed.

Because there are no medical tests to confirm a diagnosis, the only definitive way to treat it is to follow a completely gluten-free diet for a few weeks and then to reintroduce gluten into the diet. If the symptoms return after digestion of gluten, then nonceliac gluten intolerance can be confirmed and a completely gluten-free diet will need to be followed in order to feel well.

Wheat Allergy

Having a wheat allergy differs from having celiac disease. An allergic reaction to wheat will usually appear within minutes or hours after eating wheat or foods containing wheat, whereas in celiac disease the symptoms can differ and take longer to develop.

Symptoms of wheat allergy may include one or a combination of the following:

• difficulty breathing, wheezing, coughing, or a runny nose

• eczema, hives, or other skin rashes

• itchy, red, swollen, or watery eyes

• abdominal pain

• nausea, diarrhea, and/or vomiting

• swelling of the lips, tongue, or face

• a severe, systemic allergic reaction known as anaphylactic shock, which is a serious life-threatening condition that requires immediate medical treatment.

The majority of gluten-free products are suitable for those with a wheat allergy, although sometimes only the gluten is removed in the manufacturing process. Therefore, it is always necessary to use caution and check labels carefully.

Dermatitis Herpetiformis

Dermatitis herpetiformis (also referred to as DH) is a blistering skin condition related to celiac disease, however, it is much rarer. It is characterized by extremely itchy bumps and blisters that arise on normal or reddened skin and is most often found on the scalp, shoulders, buttocks, elbows, and knees. Like celiac disease, it involves antibodies and intolerance to gluten. There is a genetic disposition for this disease and it often affects more males than females. Diagnosis involves examining the skin for immunoglobulin A (IgA) and if found, normal testing for celiac disease is used to confirm the condition. It, too, is controlled by following a completely gluten-free diet.

Lactose Intolerance and the Association with Celiac Disease

Lactose is broken down by an enzyme called lactase, which is found in the lining of the small intestine. When the lining is damaged, it does not make enough lactase so lactose intolerance can occur. However, once a gluten-free diet is introduced, the small intestine is allowed to heal and the normal breakdown of lactose returns. Therefore, lactose intolerance can be a temporary problem. It is important that a discussion with a Registered Dietician (RD) takes place before eliminating lactose from a diet because this will reduce the calcium intake.

Gluten-Free and Hidden Gluten

Once diagnosed and following a gluten-free diet, many people may start to feel better almost immediately and continue to improve as their damaged small intestine is repaired and they remain gluten-free. It is important to note that it can take some time for this to occur. There are some who cannot understand why the gluten-free diet is not working for them. The simple answer to this is that hidden gluten can be found in unsuspecting food products and so gluten can unknowingly be being digested. Because gluten is most commonly found in flour, removing baked products, such as bread, cakes, and cookies, from a diet is perceived by many as following a gluten-free diet; however, this is not the case. Gluten is used in many processed products and is hidden in everyday foods. Celiacs should avoid wheat, rye, barley, and spelt.

Although oats contain gluten, it is uncertain whether they should be avoided by celiacs because oat gluten is from a different family of grains. However, because it is difficult to prevent cross-contamination by wheat in the production process, celiacs are advised to avoid oats unless it is stated that they are gluten-free. Celiacs should also be careful when a product states that it is wheat-free, because this does not necessarily mean that it is gluten-free. It is always better to be safe than sorry, so if you are not sure if a product is gluten-free, it is better to avoid it.

Today, campaigners with celiac disease are seeking new labeling regulations to make it much easier for celiacs to purchase gluten-free products. In many European countries, a product can be labeled gluten-free, but it must have less than 20 parts per million of gluten, regarded as a safe level for people with problems digesting gluten. Compaigners in the United States are supporting similar legislation to be passed by the U.S. Food and Drug Administration (USDA). In other countries, the manufacturer must state if wheat, rye, oats, and barley have been used in their product. Ingredients that have been made from cereals that contain gluten, such as glucose syrup, maltodextrin, and distilled ingredients, are now processed to remove the gluten so are, therefore, gluten-free. Other countries are also establishing new laws and legislation with regards to the labeling of gluten-free products. It is hoped that standardized labeling regulations will soon be adopted in the United States on a voluntary basis. This means that a product could be gluten-free, although not labeled as such, but at least if there is a label saying gluten-free, the food product would have to have followed standardized guidelines.

Gluten-Free Foods

The following foods are all gluten-free:

- meat and poultry

- fish and shellfish

- beans and other legumes

- dairy products (milk, cream, cheese, and plain yogurt)

- fresh vegetables

- fresh fruit

- eggs

- corn and cornmeal (maize)

- fats (including butter, margarine, and oil)

- rice and wild rice

- rice noodles

- soy and plain tofu

- nuts and seeds

- sugar and honey

- molasses, corn syrup, and maple syrup

- vanilla extract

- fresh herbs and spices

- tomato paste

- fresh and dried yeast

- preserves and marmalades

- liquors (including whiskey and malt whiskey), wine, champagne, port, sherry, liqueurs, and hard cider.

Hidden Ingredients on Food Labels

On food labels these items may contain gluten:

- wheat/whole-wheat
- wheat bran
- wheat germ
- wheat starch
- barley/scotch barley
- bran
- bread crumbs
- bulgur wheat
- cereal extract
- couscous
- farina
- flour
- whole-wheat flour
- whole-grain flour
- modified starch
- rolled oats
- oatmeal
- rusk
- rye flour
- semolina
- spelt
- khorasan wheat (Kamut®)
- vegetable protein
- vegetable gum
- vegetable starch.

Hidden Gluten in Foods

The following foods may contain gluten, however, there are gluten-free alternatives to many:

- communion wafers
- commercial ice creams
- frozen yogurts
- cheese spreads
- sour cream
- nondairy creamer
- ketchup and some sauces
- dry-roasted nuts
- licorice
- candies and confectionary
- potato chips
- canned baked beans
- canned or packaged soups

- commercial salad dressings and mayonnaise
- some spice mixes
- mustard
- some marinades
- soy sauce
- frozen fries
- teriyaki sauce
- pretzels
- Bombay mix
- white pepper
- commercial bouillon
- powdered gravy and sauce mixes
- frozen meals
- hamburgers
- sausages
- processed meat
- hot dogs
- instant cocoa mix
- malted milk drinks
- beer, lager, stout, or ale
- some carbonated drinks
- natural supplements and vitamins
- body lotions and creams
- toothpastes
- medicines
- makeup and lipsticks
- commercial play-dough mixes.

NB All serving suggestions in the recipes (e.g. ice cream) are assumed to be gluten-free.

Cross Contamination

Cross contamination can occur very easily in the kitchen. Toasters, broilers, pans, cutting boards, utensils, appliances, and oils that were used for preparing or cooking foods containing gluten may still have traces of gluten in them that can contaminate your gluten-free food. It is essential that a strict cleaning program is adhered to in order to eliminate the risk of cross contamination. Cooking oil that has been used to deep-fry foods containing gluten or coated with a gluten-containing product, such as bread crumbs, should never be reused to fry gluten-free food. Be careful when baking with ordinary flour because residues of flour can remain in the air for up to 24 hours and settle on counters and gluten-free food, such as fresh fruit. It is also important to be can be passed from knives used for spreading on nongluten-free bread. Gluten-free foods should be stored separately in the kitchen, separate cutting boards should be used, and a separate toaster should be used to make gluten-free toast. Gluten can also be found in medicines, vitamins and supplements, lipstick, make-up, toothpaste, and body lotions and creamsm so it is important to keep this in mind when using these products and to ask for gluten-free alternatives. It can also be found in play-dough mixes made for children.

Hidden Gluten When Eating Out

Some restaurants today offer gluten-free items on their menus and, if not, many good chefs are now willing to provide a gluten-free alternative on request. However, this is not always the case and catering professionals need to be better informed with regards to gluten-free products and cooking. Hidden gluten is in many prepared and processed foods, such as sauces and gravy. When eating out, therefore, it is essential that you do not eat anything that is cooked with sauces, dressings, or creams unless it is stated as being gluten-free on the menu. If in any doubt, the best way to reduce the risk is to keep your food as plain as possible and to ask for any creams, dressings, or sauces to be removed from the meal. It is also better to ask for the meat, poultry, or fish to be boiled, steamed, or

cooked in olive oil to prevent cross contamination. If gluten-free pasta or noodles are being served, make sure that they are cooked in clean water that has not been used to cook normal pasta. Fries are a common source of cross contamination and hidden gluten because they are cooked in oil that has been used to fry nongluten-free foods and gluten is often added in the manufacturing process. Be cautious also when ordering desserts, ice creams, frozen yogurts, and custards that may contain gluten.

Gluten-Free Alternatives

Wheat flour performs a range of functions, such as thickening, binding, changing texture, absorbing moisture, and adding flavor to the product. There is no single alternative to wheat flour that can replicate all these functions. Therefore, it is commonly suggested that you mix or use a combination of several flours or starches when making a substitute for wheat flour. Different flour mixes are suggested, depending upon the recipe. There is no one ideal mixture for all recipes and it is often necessary to experiment and customize the flour mix to suit the recipe. A wide variety of gluten-free flours, starches, and baking aids can be used to produce high-quality food, although it is often a case of trial and error when baking gluten-free products.

Baking without gluten can be a challenge because gluten provides important properties to various types of baked products, such as cakes, pastries, breads, and cookies. Gluten is the substance that adds the texture to baking products and it is needed for its gas-retaining ability so that a lighter consistency is produced. Gluten-free bread is possibly the most difficult product to bake but, with experimentation, it can be achieved.

Eggs are the most common binder in gluten-free baking because they replace many of the functions of gluten. Binding can also be assisted by adding cream cheese to a sweet pastry dough or cheese to unsweetened dough. Other additives can be used to replace the gas that is lost when gluten-free flours are used instead of wheat flours.

The most popular additive today is xanthan gum which, used in small quantities, can imitate the spring in bread, bind pastry, and prevent cookies from becoming too crumbly. Xanthan gum can be bought in supermarkets, health food stores, and online. Because there is no gluten to develop in gluten-free flours, kneading time will be greatly reduced during preparation. Lost moisture is also a major factor in gluten-free baking; however, this can be improved by using products such as glycerin, oil, honey, or syrup or adding plain yogurt or buttermilk to the recipe. Chocolate, fruit, spices, vanilla, and nuts are all excellent ingredients for adding flavor and improving texture.

It is important to cover and store gluten-free baked products properly because they quickly lose moisture. Store them in the refrigerator, in an airtight container, or in the freezer (if suitable) to prevent this from happening. Gluten-free baked products can be warmed for a short time in the oven or for a few moments in the microwave prior to eating to improve the texture.

Gluten-Free Flour Blends

Fortunately, gluten-free all-purpose flour blends and gluten-free bread mixes are now available to buy. Gluten-free flour blends are a general-purpose mix best used for cookies and pastry and good used with gluten-free baking powder for cakes and certain breads. Gluten-free bread mixes are used primarily for breads but are suitable for some pastries. Gluten-free flour mixes have been tried and tested to give excellent results and are often a good starting ground for gluten-free baking. However, many different types of flours are gluten-free and, when combined, they can make an excellent substitute for wheat flour in baking. These can all be bought in supermarkets, health food stores, and online.

Gluten-Free Flours and Starches

Amaranth

Amaranth flour is made from the seed of the amaranth plant. It has a pleasant peppery flavor and helps to add nutritional value, improve structure, and provide binding. It is best used in conjunction with other gluten-free flours.

Arrowroot

Arrowroot flour is ground from the root of the arrowroot plant. It is similar to cornstarch and it is used as a thickener in baking and sauces.

Brown Rice Flour

Brown rice flour is heavier and more nutritious than white rice flour. It has a nutty taste and it can add texture. It is best used in conjunction with other gluten-free flours.

Buckwheat

Buckwheat, despite the name, does not contain wheat. It has a strong, bitter flavor and is ideal for pancakes or yeast breads in conjunction with other gluten-free flours.

Chia

Chia flour is made from ground chia seeds. It is highly nutritious and has become very popular in recent years. It is best used in conjunction with other gluten-free flours to make flatbreads.

Cornstarch

This is made from very finely ground corn. It is bland in flavor but it is an excellent thickener that is often used in baking. It is sometimes referred to as cornflour.

Flaxseed (or Linseed)

This has a nutty, strong flavor and it also adds color. It retains moisture and helps to provide a spring to baked goods.

Chickpea Flour

Also called besan flour, chickpea flour is made from ground chickpeas. It is often used in Indian cooking for various types of breads, such as flatbreads.

Hemp

Hemp flour has a nutty flavor and is best used in conjunction with other gluten-free flours.

Millet

This has a powdery texture and is similar in color to cornmeal. It has a sweet flavor and is often used in muffins and flatbreads.

Nut Flours (including Almond, Chestnut, Hazelnut, Pecan, and Walnut)

Nut flours are used in conjunction with other gluten-free flours. They add flavor, texture, and nutritional value to baked goods.

Cornmeal/Polenta

This can be added to baked goods to provide color, increase moisture, and improve flavor. It is often used for muffins and bread.

Potato Flour

This should not be confused with potato starch. Potato flour has a strong flavor and is heavy, so use it sparingly in recipes.

Potato Starch

This is weak in flavor, but it helps to retain moisture and provides a soft light texture to baked goods.

Quinoa

This has a slightly mild nutty flavor. It is an excellent source of nutrition and is suitable for cakes, cookies, and breads.

Sorghum

This has a nutty, sweet flavor and is best used in conjunction with other gluten-free flours.

Soy

Soy flour is best used in conjunction with other gluten-free flours. It is used as a thickener or for its nutty taste.

Teff

This is a grain native to North Africa. It tastes very similar to hazelnuts and it is often used to add nutritional value to baked goods.

Tapioca Flour

Also called cassava flour, it has a sweet flavor and is used to add texture and color in baked goods. It is best used in conjunction with other gluten-free flours.

White Rice Flour

This is neutral in flavor and is not as nutritious as brown rice flour. It can be used alone or in conjunction with other gluten-free flours.

Gluten-Free Flour Blends and Mixes

For the purpose of convenience, the majority of the recipes in this book have been developed using commercially made, premixed flour blends. It is important that only the stated flour is used when trying the recipe at home because substituting the wrong one will affect the final outcome of the baked product.

Although it is convenient to have commercially made, premixed gluten-free flour blends at home, it may be more economical to make your own gluten-free flour mixes. These mixes can be made in bulk by doubling or tripling a recipe and stored or frozen until required. Making your own mixes also means you can customize them to suit your own palate.

There are a number of homemade flour mixes that can be achieved by combining a mixture of different gluten-free flours and starches. It is important to keep in mind that because gluten-free flour does not behave in the same way as wheat flour, a gluten-free mix may work well for one recipe but may not suit another.

Gluten-Free All Purpose Flour Mix

1½ cups sorghum flour or brown rice flour

1¾ cups tapioca flour

½ cup almond flour

1 teaspoon xanthan gum

Gluten-Free Self-Rising Flour Mix

To make self-rising flour simply add 1½ teaspoons of gluten-free

baking powder per 2 cups of the gluten-free all-purpose flour mix

Gluten-Free Cake Flour Mix

1½ cups brown rice flour

1⅓ cups plus 1 tablespoon sorghum flour

1¾ cups plus 2 tablespoons tapioca flour

Gluten-Free Bread Flour Mix

2⅓ cups soybean flour

¾ cup tapioca flour

1¾ cups potato flour

1¼ cups cornstarch

1 teaspoon xanthan gum

Chapter 1
Cupcakes & Muffins

raspberry & white chocolate cupcakes

Prep Time: 20 minutes   Cook Time: 18–20 minutes
Per cupcake: 371 cal/19g fat/7g saturated fat/50g carbs/37g sugar/0.4g salt

makes 12

2 eggs

¾ cup granulated sugar

1 teaspoon glycerin

1¼ cups gluten-free,
wheat-free self-rising flour

2½ tablespoons rice flour

½ teaspoon xanthan gum

1 teaspoon gluten-free
baking powder

3½ tablespoons almond meal
(ground almonds)

¼ cup gluten-free white
chocolate chips

½ cup sunflower oil

¼ cup milk

¼ cup light cream

½ teaspoon vanilla extract

25–30 fresh or frozen
raspberries

frosting (optional)

1¾ cups confectioners' sugar

5½ tablespoons butter,
softened

⅓ cup cream cheese

1 tablespoon milk
or light cream

fresh raspberries,
to decorate

1. Preheat the oven to 350°F. Line a 12-cup muffin pan with cupcake liners.

2. Beat the eggs, sugar, and glycerin in a large bowl until thick and fluffy. Sift the flours, xanthan gum, baking powder, and almond meal into a separate bowl.

3. Add the dry mixture to the wet mixture and fold in the chocolate chips. Add the oil, milk, cream, and vanilla extract and beat together to form a smooth batter.

4. Divide the batter among the cupcake liners, then press two raspberries into the center of each cupcake.

5. Bake in the preheated oven for 18–20 minutes, until well risen and golden. Remove from the oven and cool on a wire rack.

6. To make the frosting, beat together all the ingredients in a large bowl until thick. Place in a pastry bag and decorate each cupcake when completely cool.

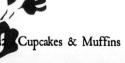

chocolate & macadamia nut cupcakes

Prep Time: 25 minutes   Cook Time: 25–30 minutes
Per cupcake: 317 cal/21g fat/10g saturated fat/30g carbs/17g sugar/0.6g salt

makes 12

1 cup granulated sugar

½ teaspoon glycerin

1½ sticks butter, softened

4 eggs, beaten

⅔ cup gluten-free unsweetened cocoa powder

1⅓ cups gluten-free, wheat-free, self-rising flour

¼ teaspoon gluten-free baking powder

¼ teaspoon xanthan gum

½ cup chopped macadamia nuts

1. Preheat the oven to 350°F. Line a 12-cup muffin pan with cupcake liners.

2. Cream together the sugar, glycerin, and butter in a large bowl. Mix in the eggs slowly, one at a time.

3. Sift the cocoa powder, flour, baking powder, and xanthan gum into the creamed mixture and mix gently together. Carefully fold in half of the macadamia nuts with 3 tablespoons warm water.

4. Divide the batter among the cupcake liners and sprinkle with the remaining nuts.

5. Bake in the preheated oven for 25–30 minutes, or until the nuts are golden and the muffins spring back when lightly touched in the middle. Remove the cupcakes from the oven and cool on a wire rack.

carrot cupcakes with almond & lime frosting

Prep Time: 20 minutes   Cook Time: 18–20 minutes
Per cupcake: 400 cal/21g fat/7g saturated fat/54g carbs/42g sugar/0.4g salt

makes 9

½ cup firmly packed light brown sugar

⅓ cup sunflower oil

2 eggs

a pinch of saffron strands, crumbled

1 cup gluten-free, wheat-free self-rising flour, sifted

½ teaspoon gluten-free baking powder

1 teaspoon xanthan gum

½ teaspoon allspice

2 cups shredded carrot

⅓ cup chopped walnuts

frosting

½ cup cream cheese

3 tablespoons butter, softened

2 tablespoons almond meal (ground almonds)

zest of 2 limes

2 cups confectioners' sugar

¼ cup slivered almonds, to decorate

1. Preheat the oven to 350°F. Line 9 cups of a 12-cup muffin pan with cupcake liners.

2. Beat together the sugar, oil, eggs, and saffron in a large bowl until creamy. Then add the sifted flour, baking powder, xanthan gum, allspice, shredded carrot, and chopped walnuts.

3. Divide the batter among the cupcake liners and bake the cupcakes in the preheated oven for 18–20 minutes, until well risen and golden. Remove from the oven and cool on a wire rack.

4. To make the frosting, process the cream cheese, butter, almond meal, lime zest, and confectioners' sugar until fluffy in a food processor.

5. Place the frosting in a pastry bag and decorate each cupcake with swirls of frosting when completely cool. Finish by sprinkling the slivered almonds over the cupcakes.

banana cupcakes with maple cream frosting

Prep Time: 20 minutes   Cook Time: 25–30 minutes
Per cupcake: 480 cal/20g fat/12g saturated fat/75g carbs/56g sugar/0.7g salt

makes 12

1 stick butter

¾ cup firmly packed light brown sugar

2 eggs

½ cup light cream

2 tablespoons maple syrup

1 tablespoon glycerin

1¾ cups gluten-free self-rising flour, sifted

½ teaspoon gluten-free baking soda

2 cups mashed banana

frosting

4 tablespoons butter, softened

½ cup cream cheese

3 cups confectioners' sugar

¼ cup maple syrup, plus extra to serve (optional)

1. Preheat the oven to 350°F. Line a 12-cup muffin pan with cupcake liners.

2. In a food processor, process the butter and brown sugar until fluffy. Add the eggs and then slowly mix in the cream, maple syrup, glycerin, sifted flour, and baking soda. Fold in the mashed bananas.

3. Divide the batter among the cupcake liners and bake the cupcakes in the preheated oven for 25–30 minutes, until well risen and golden. Remove from the oven and place on a wire rack to cool.

4. To make the frosting, process the butter, cream cheese, confectioners' sugar, and maple syrup until fluffy in a food processor.

5. Place the frosting in a pastry bag and pipe the frosting onto each cupcake when completely cool. Serve with maple syrup, if using.

fudge-frosted chocolate cupcakes

Prep Time: 10–15 minutes   Cook Time: 15–20 minutes
Per cupcake: 558 cal/28g fat/16g saturated fat/76g carbs/61g sugar/0.7g salt

makes 12

2 ounces gluten-free semisweet dark chocolate, broken into pieces

1½ sticks butter

¾ cup granulated sugar

3 eggs

½ teaspoon vanilla extract

½ teaspoon glycerin

1⅓ cups gluten-free, wheat-free self-rising flour

½ teaspoon gluten-free baking powder

1 teaspoon xanthan gum

½ cup almond meal (ground almonds)

frosting

3 ounces gluten-free semisweet dark chocolate, broken into pieces

1 stick butter

3½ cups confectioners' sugar

¾ cup milk

½ teaspoon vanilla extract

1. Preheat the oven to 350°F. Line a 12-cup muffin pan with cupcake liners.

2. Melt the chocolate in a heatproof bowl set over a saucepan of simmering water. In a separate bowl, beat together the butter and granulated sugar, then mix in the eggs, one at a time, and add the vanilla extract and glycerin. Once the chocolate has cooled slightly, add the butter and egg mixture to the melted chocolate.

3. Sift the flour, baking powder, and xanthan gum in a bowl and add the almond meal. Then stir the dry mixture gently into the chocolate and egg mixture.

4. Spoon the batter into the cupcake liners and bake the cupcakes in the preheated oven for 15–20 minutes, or until a toothpick inserted into the center comes out clean. Remove from the oven and cool on a wire rack.

5. To make the frosting, melt the chocolate and butter in a heatproof bowl set over a saucepan of simmering water. Mix the confectioners' sugar, half the milk, and the vanilla extract in a separate bowl and slowly add the chocolate mixture. Add the rest of the milk to get the desired consistency.

6. Place the frosting in a pastry bag and decorate each cupcake when completely cool.

blueberry & oatmeal muffins

Prep Time: 15 minutes   Cook Time: 20–25 minutes
Per muffin: 260 cal/11.5g fat/1.5g saturated fat/38g carbs/15g sugar/0.4g salt

makes 9

1 cup pure
orange juice

⅔ cup gluten-free,
wheat-free rolled oats

½ cup granulated sugar

1⅔ cups gluten-free,
wheat-free all-purpose
flour, sifted

½ teaspoon xanthan gum

1½ teaspoons gluten-free
baking powder

½ teaspoon gluten-free
baking soda

½ teaspoon cinnamon

¼ teaspoon allspice

½ cup vegetable oil

1 egg, beaten

1 teaspoon glycerin

1¼ cups blueberries

raw brown sugar, to sprinkle

1. Preheat the oven to 350°F. Line a deep 9-cup muffin pan with muffin cups.

2. Add the orange juice to the rolled oats and mix well in a bowl.

3. In a separate bowl, mix together the sugar, flour, xanthan gum, baking powder, baking soda, and spices. Add the oil, egg, and glycerin to the dry mixture and mix well. Then add the oat mixture and blueberries and fold these in gently.

4. Divide the batter among the muffin cups and sprinkle with raw sugar.

5. Bake the muffins in the preheated oven for 20–25 minutes, or until a toothpick inserted in a muffin comes out clean. Remove from the oven and cool on a wire rack.

honey & lemon corn muffins

Prep Time: 15 minutes   Cook Time: 18–20 minutes
Per muffin: 159 cal/5.5g fat/1g saturated fat/25g carbs/8.5g sugar/0.25g salt

makes 12

1 cup gluten-free, wheat-free all-purpose flour

¾ cup plus 2 tablespoons gluten-free, wheat-free cornmeal

¼ cup granulated sugar

2 teaspoons gluten-free baking powder

¼ teaspoon xanthan gum

1 egg

juice and zest of ½ lemon

¼ cup vegetable oil

1 cup milk

2 tablespoons honey

1 tablespoon glycerin

1. Preheat the oven to 350°F. Line a 12-cup muffin pan with muffin cups.

2. Place the flour, cornmeal, sugar, baking powder, and xanthan gum into a bowl and mix together well.

3. In a separate bowl, mix together all the remaining liquid ingredients. Add the liquid mixture to the dry mixture and fold in gently.

4. Spoon the batter into the muffin cups and bake the muffins in the preheated oven for 18–20 minutes, until well risen and golden. Remove from the oven and cool on a wire rack.

apple & cinnamon bran muffins

Prep Time: 15 minutes   Cook Time: 20–25 minutes
Per muffin: 300 cal/8g fat/1.5g saturated fat/52g carbs/29g sugar/0.3g salt

makes 12

¼ cup vegetable oil

1 tablespoon glycerin

¾ cup applesauce

2 eggs

½ teaspoon vanilla extract

¼ cup honey

¼ cup milk

2⅓ cups gluten-free, wheat-free all-purpose flour

1¼ cups gluten-free, wheat-free oat bran

⅔ cup ground flaxseed

1 teaspoon gluten-free baking powder

½ teaspoon gluten-free baking soda

½ teaspoon xanthan gum

1 teaspoon cinnamon

¼ teaspoon allspice

¾ cup firmly packed light brown sugar

¾ cup raisins and golden raisins

1. Preheat the oven to 350°F. Line a 12-cup muffin pan with muffin cups.

2. In a large bowl, beat together the vegetable oil, glycerin, applesauce, eggs, vanilla extract, honey, and milk. In a separate bowl, mix together all the dry ingredients, then add the liquid mixture and stir well.

3. Divide the batter among the muffin cups. Bake the muffins in the preheated oven for 20–25 minutes, or until a toothpick inserted into a muffin comes out clean. Remove from the oven and cool on a wire rack.

chocolate & vanilla whoopie pies

Prep Time: 15 minutes   Cook Time: 8–10 minutes
Per pie: 350 cal/22g fat/13g saturated fat/37g carbs/26g sugar/0.7g salt

makes 10

1 stick butter,
plus extra for greasing

½ cup firmly packed light
brown sugar

2 eggs

2 teaspoons vanilla extract

1 teaspoon glycerin

1 cup gluten-free, wheat-free
all-purpose flour

1 teaspoon gluten-free
baking powder

½ teaspoon gluten-free
baking soda

1 teaspoon xanthan gum

⅓ cup gluten-free
unsweetened cocoa
powder

⅔ cup milk

buttercream

6 tablespoons butter,
softened

1 cup confectioners' sugar,
plus extra for sprinkling

2 tablespoons heavy cream

1. Preheat the oven to 400°F. Grease two large baking sheets and line with parchment paper or silicone paper.

2. Cream the butter, sugar, eggs, vanilla extract, and glycerin in a bowl. Sift all the dry ingredients into the bowl and fold into the mixture. Slowly add just enough milk to make a smooth batter.

3. Use two teaspoons to shape 20 walnut-size balls of the batter and place them well apart on the prepared baking sheets.

4. Bake in the preheated oven, one sheet at a time, for 8–10 minutes, or until just risen and firm to the touch. Cool on a wire rack.

5. To make the buttercream, whip together the butter, confectioners' sugar, and cream until creamy.

6. To assemble, spread or pipe the buttercream filling on the flat side of half of the cakes. Top with the rest of the cakes. Arrange on a serving plate and sift confectioners' sugar over the pies.

rocky road cake pops

Prep Time: 15 minutes, plus chilling time   Cook Time: No cooking
Per pop: 287 cal/18g fat/9g saturated fat/31g carbs/25g sugar/0.3g salt

makes 40

1 chocolate brownie cake
(hazelnuts and white
chocolate optional—
see recipe on page 64)

1½ tablespoons light cream

2 cups confectioners' sugar

4 tablespoons butter,
softened

1 cup cream cheese

12 ounces gluten-free
semisweet dark chocolate,
broken into pieces

toppings

1 bowl of mini
marshmallows

1 bowl of chopped walnuts

1 bowl of gluten-free
cookie crumbs

1. Make the brownie cake as per recipe on page 64 and let cool. Crumble the cake into a large bowl using your fingertips.

2. Mix together the cream, confectioners' sugar, butter, and cream cheese until smooth and creamy. Add the brownie mixture and stir with a spatula.

3. Knead the mix with your hands to form a dough (if the mix is too dry, add a little more cream). Refrigerate until the dough is firm to the touch.

4. Line one to two baking sheets with parchment paper. Roll out 1–2 inch cake balls from the dough and place on the baking sheets. Insert a lollypop stick into each ball. Put the baking sheets into the freezer for 30 minutes.

5. Melt the chocolate in a heatproof bowl set over a saucepan of simmering water, stirring well as it melts. When the cake balls have hardened, remove from freezer and dip and cover each one with the melted chocolate. Sprinkle on the marshmallows, chopped walnuts, and cookie crumbs. Return to the baking sheets to set.

buttermilk & golden raisin scones

Prep Time: 20 minutes   Cook Time: 15–20 minutes
Per scone: 181 cal/6.5g fat/3.5g saturated fat/28g carbs/8g sugar/0.6g salt

makes 10

1²⁄₃ cups gluten-free, wheat-free all-purpose flour, sifted, plus extra for dusting

¹⁄₃ cup rice flour, sifted

1 tablespoon gluten-free baking powder

2 teaspoons xanthan gum

3 tablespoons confectioners' sugar

3¹⁄₂ tablespoons butter, cubed, plus extra for greasing

1 cup plain yogurt

¹⁄₄ cup buttermilk

¹⁄₃ cup golden raisins

1 egg, beaten, for glazing

1. Preheat the oven to 400°F. Grease a large baking sheet and line it with parchment paper.

2. Sift the flours, baking powder, xanthan gum, and confectioners' sugar into a large bowl. Add the butter and, using your fingertips, rub it into the dry mixture until the mixture resembles fine bread crumbs.

3. Add the yogurt, buttermilk, and golden raisins, and mix to form a soft dough ball.

4. Knead the dough on a floured surface and roll out to a thickness of about ³⁄₄–1¹⁄₄ inches. Cut out 8–10 circles with a pastry cutter and place on the baking sheet. Brush each scone with the beaten egg to glaze.

5. Bake in the preheated oven for 15–20 minutes, until well risen and golden. Remove from the oven and let cool on a wire rack.

vanilla, cinnamon & chocolate donuts

Prep Time: 1 hour   Cook Time: 20–25 minutes
Per doughnut: 190 cal/10g fat/3g saturated fat/22g carbs/10g sugar/1.8g salt

makes 24

yeast mix

½ cup lukewarm water

2¼ teaspoons active dry yeast

1½ teaspoons honey

donuts

2⅓ cups gluten-free, wheat-free self-rising flour

⅓ cup brown rice flour

¼ teaspoon xanthan gum

¼ teaspoon gluten-free baking powder

¼ teaspoon ground nutmeg

¼ teaspoon ground cinnamon

4 tablespoons butter, softened

1 cup almond meal (ground almonds)

½ teaspoon vanilla extract

1 egg plus 1 egg yolk

1 tablespoon buttermilk

24 gluten-free semisweet chocolate drops

vegetable oil, for greasing and frying

¾ cup superfine sugar or granulated sugar, to dust

3 tablespoons ground cinnamon, to dust

chocolate sauce, to serve

vanilla ice cream, to serve

1. To make the yeast mix, add the lukewarm water to the dry yeast in a bowl and stir in the honey. Let stand at room temperature for 15 minutes, until frothy.

2. Sift the flours, xanthan gum, baking powder, nutmeg, and cinnamon into a large bowl. Rub the butter into the flour mixture using your fingertips, until the mixture resembles fine bread crumbs. Stir in the almonds, vanilla extract, egg, egg yolk, and buttermilk. Pour in the yeast mix and stir well to form a dough, adding a little more water, if required. Let stand in a warm place until doubled in size.

3. Cover a baking sheet with a sheet of parchment paper and grease the paper. Form 24 small dough balls and insert a chocolate drop inside each one. Place them onto the prepared baking sheet and cover with greased plastic wrap for 40 minutes.

4. Make the sugar dusting for the donuts by mixing the together the superfine sugar and ground cinnamon.

5. Heat enough oil to just cover the donuts in a large saucepan or deep-fryer to 350°–375°F, or until a cube of bread browns in 30 seconds. Cook the donuts in the hot oil, three to four at a time, for 2–3 minutes on each side, until golden brown.

6. Drain on paper towels and roll in the sugar dusting. Serve with chocolate sauce and vanilla ice cream.

Chapter 2
Cookies & Bars

apricot & coconut bars

Prep Time: 25 minutes   Cook Time: 2–3 hours chilling
Per bar: 252 cal/15g fat/8.5g saturated fat/28g carbs/17g sugar/0.5g salt

makes 24

1 pound gluten-free, wheat-free graham crackers

2 cups dried apricots

2 tablespoons sesame seeds

2¼ sticks butter, plus extra for greasing

2 tablespoons honey

1 (14-ounce can) condensed milk

⅓ cup unsweetened dry coconut

1 tablespoon slivered almonds

1. Grease a 10 x 7-inch rectangular baking pan and line it with parchment paper.

2. In a food processor, process the graham crackers on pulse until they are crushed. Set aside. Add the apricots to the processor and process until finely chopped.

3. Place the apricots and crumbs in a large bowl and add the sesame seeds.

4. Place the butter, honey, and condensed milk in a heavy saucepan and cook over low heat, stirring until the mixture is smooth and melted. Continue to cook over low heat, stirring for 3–4 minutes, or until the mixture has thickened slightly. Remove from the heat, cool slightly, and then add the crushed crackers, apricots, and sesame seeds.

5. Place the mixture on the baking sheet and smooth out with a spatula to fit the sheet. Sprinkle with the coconut and slivered almonds and refrigerate for 2–3 hours, until set.

6. When set, cut into bars. The bars can be stored in an airtight container for up to one week.

chewy chocolate & mixed berry bars

Prep Time: 30 minutes   Cook Time: 30 minutes
Per bar: 207 cal/7g fat/4g saturated fat/32g carbs/24g sugar/0.3g salt

makes 16

1 cup firmly packed light brown sugar

1 stick butter, plus extra for greasing

2 eggs, beaten

1 cup gluten-free, wheat-free all-purpose flour

¼ teaspoon xanthan gum

1 teaspoon gluten-free baking powder

3 tablespoons gluten-free unsweetened cocoa powder

¾ cup usnweetened dry coconut

1 cup mixed dried berries

fudge topping

3 tablespoons gluten-free unsweetened cocoa powder

1¼ cups confectioners' sugar

½ teaspoon vanilla extract

1 tablespoon butter, melted

2 tablespoons warm water

1. Preheat the oven to 350°F. Grease an 8 x 12-inch baking pan and line with parchment paper.

2. Cream together the sugar and butter in a large bowl until pale and fluffy. Add the eggs gradually, one at a time, mixing well after each addition. Sift the flour, xanthan gum, baking powder, and cocoa into the egg mixture and fold in gently. Add the coconut and the berries and mix well.

3. Spoon the batter into the baking pan and smooth with a rubber spatula.

4. Bake in the preheated oven for 30 minutes, until well risen. Remove from the oven and cool on a wire rack.

5. To make the fudge topping, sift the cocoa powder and confectioners' sugar into a bowl. Add the vanilla extract, melted butter, and warm water and mix until the mixture is easy to spread.

6. Spread on top of the baked cake when cooled completely and refrigerate. When set, cut into bars. The bars can be stored in an airtight container for up to two weeks.

breakfast cereal bars

Prep Time: 10 minutes   Cook Time: 30–35 minutes
Per bar: 240 cal/14g fat/7g saturated fat/22g carbs/12g sugar/0.3g salt

makes 12

1 stick butter, softened,
plus extra for greasing

2 tablespoons packed light
brown sugar

2 tablespoons light
corn syrup

2 eggs, beaten

2½ cups millet flakes

½ cup raisins

⅓ cup quinoa

⅓ cup dried cranberries

½ cup golden raisins

2 tablespoons pumpkin seeds

2½ tablespoons sesame seeds

3 tablespoons chopped
walnuts

½ cup unsweetened
dry coconut

1. Preheat the oven to 350°F. Grease a10 x 7-inch baking pan and line it with parchment paper.

2. Beat together the butter, sugar, and syrup until creamy in a large bowl. Add all the remaining ingredients and stir well until combined.

3. Place the batter in the pan and level the surface with a rubber spatula.

4. Bake in the preheated oven for 30–35 minutes, or until golden brown.

5. When cool, invert onto a flat surface and cut into 12 bars. The bars can be stored in an airtight container for up to one week.

rocky road snack bars

Prep Time: 10 minutes   Cook Time: 10 minutes, plus chilling time
Per bar: 290 cal/19g fat/12g saturated fat/30g carbs/22g sugar/0.3g salt

makes 16

1 stick butter,
plus extra for greasing

2 tablespoons light
corn syrup

9 ounces gluten-free
semisweet dark chocolate,
broken into pieces

22 gluten-free, wheat-free
graham crackers or
cookies (about 5½ ounces)

1⅓ cups miniature
marshmallows

6 Brazil nuts, chopped

1 cup golden raisins

1⅔ cups unsweetened
dry coconut

1. Grease a 10 x 7-inch baking pan and line it with parchment paper.

2. Put the butter, syrup, and chocolate in a heatproof bowl set over a saucepan of simmering water, making sure that the bowl does not touch the water. Melt until glossy and smooth in texture.

3. In a separate bowl, break the cookies into small pieces and add the remaining dry ingredients. Pour in the chocolate mixture and mix well.

4. Transfer the chocolate mixture to the prepared pan and smooth the surface. Chill in the refrigerator for 2–3 hours, or until firmly set.

5. When set, cut into bars. The bars can be stored in an airtight container for up to two weeks.

roasted hazelnut shortbread

Prep Time: 20 minutes   Cook Time: 10–15 minutes
Per cookie: 200 cal/14g fat/8g saturated fat/18g carbs/6g sugar/0.3g salt

makes 18

¾ cup confectioners' sugar

1½ cups gluten-free, wheat-free all-purpose flour, plus extra for dusting

½ cup gluten-free cornstarch

⅓ cup chopped roasted hazelnuts

⅓ cup almond meal (ground almonds)

2¼ sticks butter, plus extra for greasing

½ teaspoon vanilla extract

superfine sugar or granulated sugar, for sprinkling

1. Preheat the oven to 350°F. Grease one or two baking sheets and line them with parchment paper.

2. Put the dry ingredients into a bowl and rub in the butter and vanilla extract until the ingredients form a dough.

3. Invert onto a floured surface and knead slightly. Roll out to a thickness of ½ inch. Cut out 16–18 circles using a 2¾-inch cutter and place on the baking sheet.

4. Bake in the preheated oven for 10–15 minutes, until golden. Remove from the oven and dust with superfine sugar while still warm. Let cool on a wire rack.

mandarin & chocolate chip cookies

Prep Time: 15 minutes   Cook Time: 15 minutes
Per cookie: 245 cal/11g fat/6g saturated fat/35g carbs/15g sugar/0.6g salt

makes 10

4 ounces gluten-free semisweet dark chocolate

¼ cup firmly packed light brown sugar

1 tablespoon granulated sugar

5 tablespoons butter, plus extra for greasing

1 egg, beaten

2 cups gluten-free, wheat-free all-purpose flour, plus extra for dusting

½ teaspoon xanthan gum

1 tablespoon gluten-free unsweetened cocoa powder

1 teaspoon gluten-free baking soda

juice of ½ mandarin orange

zest of 2 mandarin oranges

1. Preheat the oven to 350°F. Grease a baking sheet and line with parchment paper.

2. Break or chop the chocolate into small chunks and set aside one-quarter of the chunks to top the cookies.

3. Cream together the sugars and butter in a bowl until light and fluffy. Gradually beat in the egg. Add the flour, xanthan gum, cocoa powder, baking soda, chocolate chunks, and the orange juice and zest.

4. Bring the mixture together by hand, forming a ball, and invert onto a floured surface. Divide into 8–10 circles, using about 2 tablespoons of cookie dough per ball.

5. Place the circles on a baking sheet, allowing space in between for each cookie to spread. Flatten each cookie slightly and sprinkle with the reserved chocolate chunks.

6. Bake in the preheated oven for about 15 minutes, or until just firm to the touch. Remove from the oven and let cool on a wire rack.

oatmeal & vanilla cookies

Prep Time: 20 minutes   Cook Time: 18–20 minutes
Per cookie: 192 cal/9g fat/4.5g saturated fat/28g carbs/14g sugar/0.2g salt

makes 24

1 stick butter,
plus extra for greasing

1 cup firmly packed light
brown sugar

2 eggs

1 tablespoon vanilla extract

1⅓ cups gluten-free, wheat-
free all-purpose flour

1 teaspoon xanthan gum

1½ teaspoon gluten-free
baking powder

2½ cups gluten-free
rolled oats

1 cup gluten-free semisweet
dark chocolate chips

2 tablespoons almond meal
(ground almonds)

1. Preheat the oven to 350°F. Grease one or two baking sheets and line with parchment paper.

2. Cream together the butter and sugar in a bowl using an electric mixer or in a food processor. Slowly add the eggs and vanilla extract, then slowly add the dry ingredients to the bowl and mix until well combined.

3. Divide the dough into 20–24 balls and place them on the baking sheets. Flatten each cookie using wet fingertips and press to shape.

4. Bake in the preheated oven for 18–20 minutes, until golden. Remove from the oven and let cool on the sheets. The cookies can be stored in an airtight container for up to one week.

almond & pistachio biscotti

Prep Time: 20 minutes   Cook Time: 35–42 minutes
Per biscotti: 105 cal/2.5g fat/0.5g saturated fat/17g carbs/8g sugar/trace salt

makes 40

butter, for greasing

2 teaspoon gluten-free baking powder

2¼ cups superfine sugar or granulated sugar

3⅔ cups gluten-free, wheat-free all-purpose flour

½ teaspoon xanthan gum

2 tablespoons almond meal (ground almonds)

3 extra-large eggs, beaten

⅓ cup blanched almonds, chopped

⅓ cup dried cranberries

⅔ cup chopped dried apricots

⅓ cup chopped dates

½ cup pistachio nuts

⅓ cup hazelnuts

1 teaspoon lime zest

½ teaspoon vanilla extract

1. Preheat the oven to 350°F. Grease a baking sheet and line it with parchment paper.

2. Place the baking powder, sugar, flour, xanthan gum, and almond meal in a large bowl. Add the eggs and mix well. Slowly add the chopped almonds, cranberries, apricots, dates, pistachio nuts, hazelnuts, lime zest, and vanilla extract and then mix to form a dough.

3. Roll into four cylinder shapes about 2 inches in diameter and place on the baking sheet, leaving plenty of space in between each one. Slightly press the cylinder shapes down using wet fingertips.

4. Bake in the preheated oven for 18–25 minutes, until golden. Remove from the oven and let cool. Do not turn off the oven.

5. Diagonally cut each cylinder into eight to ten 1-inch thick slices. Return the slices to the baking sheets, cut side down, and bake for an additional 7 minutes. Turn over the biscotti and cook for about 10 minutes.

6. Remove from the oven and let cool completely on a wire rack.

hazelnut & white chocolate brownies

Prep Time: 25 minutes   Cook Time: 30–35 minutes
Per brownie: 490 cal/31g fat/15g saturated fat/50g carbs/40g sugar/0.5g salt

makes 12

7½ ounces gluten-free white chocolate, broken into pieces

2 sticks butter, plus extra for greasing

1 teaspoon vanilla extract

3 eggs, beaten

1½ cups granulated sugar

1 cup gluten-free, wheat-free all-purpose flour

1 teaspoon xanthan gum

1 teaspoon gluten-free baking powder

⅓ cup gluten-free unsweetened cocoa powder

2 tablespoons almond meal (ground almonds)

½ cup gluten-free white chocolate chips

¾ cup chopped roasted hazelnuts

1. Preheat the oven to 325°F. Grease an 8 x 12-inch baking pan and line with parchment paper.

2. Put the white chocolate pieces, butter, and vanilla extract in a heatproof bowl set over a saucepan of simmering water, until melted.

3. Let the melted chocolate mixture cool a little. Cream the eggs and sugar until thick and fluffy, then fold into the chocolate mixture. Add the dry ingredients, then gently fold in.

4. Spoon the batter into the baking pan and smooth with a rubber spatula.

5. Bake in the preheated oven for 30–35 minutes, until well risen and firm to the touch. Remove from the oven and cool in the pan for about 1½ hours. Once cool, cut into 12 squares.

apricot, cranberry & chocolate chip oat bars

Prep Time: 15 minutes   Cook Time: 35 minutes
Per oat bar: 192 cal/10.5g fat/6g saturated fat/22g carbs/11g sugar/0.2g salt

makes 16

½ cup firmly packed light brown sugar

1 stick butter, softened, plus extra for greasing

2 tablespoons light corn syrup

2⅓ cups gluten-free, wheat-free rolled oats

⅓ cup cranberries

1 tablespoon sunflower seeds

⅓ cup unsweetened dry coconut

⅔ cup coarsely chopped dried apricots

¼ cup gluten-free milk chocolate chips

2 teaspoons allspice

1. Preheat the oven to 300°F. Grease a 10 x 7-inch baking pan and line it with parchment paper.

2. Put the sugar, butter, and syrup in a saucepan and heat over medium heat until the sugar has dissolved.

3. Add the rest of the ingredients to a large bowl and pour over the melted butter mixture. Mix well.

4. Put the mixture into the prepared pan and press down until smooth.

5. Bake in the preheated oven for 35 minutes, or until golden. Let cool in the sheet and then cut into pieces. The oat bars can be stored in an airtight container for up to one week (note that the oat bars are not suitable for freezing).

Chapter 3

Family & Celebration Cakes

carrot cake with lemon cream frosting

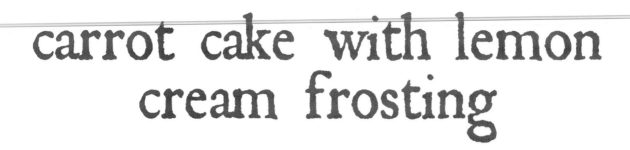

Prep Time: 20 minutes   Cook Time: 1 hr 20 minutes
Per cake: 8,339 cal/422g fat/119g saturated fat/1,059g carbs/814g sugar/10.4g salt

makes 1 cake

butter, for greasing

1 cup vegetable oil

1⅓ cups firmly packed light brown sugar

3 eggs

2 tablespoons almond meal (ground almonds)

4 cups shredded carrots

1 cup chopped walnuts

3 cups gluten-free, wheat-free self-rising flour

1 teaspoon gluten-free baking soda

1½ teaspoons allspice

frosting

4 tablespoons butter

⅔ cup cream cheese

zest of 1 lemon and juice of ½ lemon

4 cups confectioners' sugar, sifted

walnut halves, to decorate (optional)

1. Preheat the oven to 350°F. Grease an 8-inch round cake pan and line with parchment paper.

2 . In a large bowl, beat together the oil, sugar, and eggs until fluffy. Slowly fold in the rest of the ingredients.

3. Pour the batter into the cake pan and bake on the middle shelf of the preheated oven for 1 hour 20 minutes, or until a toothpick inserted in the center comes out clean.

4. Remove from the oven and cool in the pan for about 20 minutes. Transfer to a wire rack to cool completely.

5. To make the frosting, using an electric mixer, beat together the butter, cream cheese, and lemon zest and juice. Gradually add the sifted confectioners' sugar, a little at a time, until a smooth frosting forms.

6. Once the cake has cooled, spread the top of the cake with the frosting and decorate with walnuts, if desired.

chocolate fudge cake

Prep Time: 20 minutes   Cook Time: 30 minutes
Per cake: 5,879 cal/282g fat/170g saturated fat/776g carbs/642g sugar/7.1g salt

makes 1 cake

4 ounces gluten-free
semisweet dark chocolate,
broken into pieces

1 stick butter,
plus extra for greasing

1 cup firmly packed light
brown sugar

½ cup granulated sugar

1 teaspoon glycerin

2 eggs, beaten

½ cup plain yogurt

½ teaspoon vanilla extract

⅔ cup rice flour

¾ cup gluten-free, wheat-
free self-rising flour

1 teaspoon xanthan gum

1½ teaspoons gluten-free
baking powder

½ teaspoon gluten-free
baking soda

frosting

5 ounces gluten-free
semisweet dark chocolate,
broken into pieces

⅔ cup heavy cream

1 stick butter

1⅓ cups confectioners'
sugar, sifted

1. Preheat the oven to 350°F. Grease two 8-inch round cake pans and line with parchment paper.

2. Melt the chocolate in a heatproof bowl set over a ssaucepan of simmering water. In a separate bowl, cream the butter, sugars, and glycerin until fluffy and light. Slowly add the eggs, one at a time, and beat well. Add the yogurt, vanilla extract, and the cooled chocolate mixture. Fold the flours, xanthan gum, baking powder, and baking soda into the mixture gently. Add a little warm water if the batter seems too stiff.

3. Divide the batter between the two pans and bake in the preheated oven for 30 minutes, or until a toothpick inserted in the center comes out clean.

4. Remove from the oven and let cool in the pans for 30 minutes, then transfer to a wire rack to cool completely.

5. To make the frosting, melt the chocolate and cream in a heatproof bowl set over a saucepan of simmering water. Beat together the butter and confectioners' sugar in a separate bowl and then add the chocolate mixture. Beat well until it reaches a fudgelike consistency.

6. Spread the top of one sponge with some of the fudge frosting and place the other sponge on top. Spread the rest of the fudge frosting over the top and sides of the cake. Refrigerate for 30 minutes. The cake can be stored in an airtight container for three or four days.

country-style farmhouse fruitcake

Prep Time: 30 minutes   Cook Time: 1 hr–1 hr 15 minutes
Per cake: 2,608 cal/134g fat/69g saturated fat/309g carbs/194g sugar/5.4g salt

makes 1 cake

1 stick butter, plus extra for greasing

½ cup firmly packed light brown sugar

2 eggs

1 cup gluten-free, wheat-free self-rising flour, sifted

⅓ cup rice flour

1½ teaspoons gluten-free baking powder

½ teaspoon xanthan gum

2 teaspoons allspice

⅓ cup raisins

⅓ cup chopped dried apricots

1 medium Granny Smith apple, peeled, cored, and diced

¼ cup milk

2 tablespoons slivered almonds

1. Preheat the oven to 325°F. Grease a deep, 7-inch round springform cake pan and line with parchment paper.

2. Put the butter and sugar in a bowl and cream together until fluffy. Add the eggs, one at a time, stirring well. Add the flours, baking powder, xanthan gum, and allspice and mix together gently.

3. Fold in the golden raisins, dried apricots, apple, and enough of the milk to moisten the mixture.

4. Put the batter into the cake pan and level with a rubber spatula. Sprinkle the top with the slivered almonds.

5. Bake in the preheated oven for 1 hour–1 hour 15 minutes, until golden brown and firm to the touch. Remove from the oven and let cool in the pan for 20 minutes, then invert onto a wire rack. The cake can be served warm or cold.

mocha bundt cake

Prep Time: 20 minutes   Cook Time: 30 minutes
Per cake: 2,883 cal/99g fat/27g saturated fat/429g carbs/254g sugar/6.8g salt

makes 1 cake

2 eggs

3 tablespoons instant coffee granules

1 cup milk

1 cup granulated sugar

¼ cup sunflower oil

1 teaspoon glycerin

1½ teaspoons vanilla extract

1¾ cups gluten-free, wheat-free all-purpose flour

¼ cup almond meal (ground almonds)

½ teaspoon gluten-free baking powder

1 teaspoon gluten-free baking soda

1 cup gluten-free unsweetened cocoa powder

½ teaspoon salt

¾ teaspoon xanthan gum

butter, for greasing

1. Preheat the oven to 350°F. Lightly grease a 10-inch Bundt pan.

2. Beat together the eggs, coffee, milk, sugar, oil, glycerin, and vanilla extract in a large bowl.

3. In a separate bowl, mix together the flour, almond meal, baking powder, baking soda, cocoa powder, salt, and xanthan gum. Add the flour mixture to the egg mixture and stir to form a batter.

4. Transfer the batter to the prepared Bundt pan and bake on the middle shelf of the preheated oven for 30 minutes, or until a toothpick inserted in the center comes out clean.

5. Remove from the oven and let cool in the pan for 45 minutes, then invert on to a wire rack to cool completely.

layer cake with vanilla & strawberries

Prep Time: 20 minutes   Cook Time: 30–35 minutes
Per cake: 6,238 cal/457g fat/246g saturated fat/427g carbs/302g sugar/7.3g salt

makes 1 cake

2 sticks butter,
plus extra for greasing

1 cup granulated sugar

4 eggs

1 teaspoon vanilla extract

1²/₃ cups gluten-free, wheat-
free all-purpose flour

1 cup almond meal
(ground almonds)

2 teaspoons gluten-free
baking powder

¹/₃ cup of gluten-free
strawberry preserves

1 pint of strawberries,
halved

confectioners' sugar,
for dusting

vanilla cream

1¹/₂ cups heavy cream

1 teaspoon vanilla extract

1. Preheat the oven to 325°F. Grease two 8-inch cake pans and line with parchment paper.

2. Cream the butter and sugar in a large bowl. Slowly add the eggs, one at a time, and the vanilla extract, mixing well. Add the flour, almond meal, and baking powder and mix well.

3. Divide the batter between the two prepared pans and bake in the preheated oven for 30–35 minutes, or until the sponge springs back when lightly touched in the center.

4. Remove from the oven and let cool in the pans for about 10 minutes. Then invert onto a wire rack to cool completely.

5. To make the vanilla cream, whip the cream and vanilla extract in a bowl.

6. When completely cool, sandwich the cakes together with the strawberry preserves, vanilla cream, and strawberry halves. Dust the top with confectioners' sugar.

Family & Celebration Cakes

chocolate & walnut banana bread

Prep Time: 25–30 minutes   Cook Time: 40–50 minutes
Per loaf: 4,668 cal/215g fat/104g saturated fat/588g carbs/424g sugar/5.1g salt

makes 1 loaf

2 tablespoons rice flour

1¾ cups gluten-free, wheat-free all-purpose flour

1 teaspoon xanthan gum

2 teaspoons gluten-free baking powder

3 bananas, mashed

1 cup granulated sugar

1 stick butter, melted

2 eggs, beaten

½ teaspoon vanilla extract

1 cup gluten-free semisweet dark chocolate chips

½ cup chopped walnuts

unsalted butter, for greasing and to serve

1. Preheat the oven to 350°F. Grease a 9-inch loaf pan and line with parchment paper.

2. Sift the flours, xanthan gum, and baking powder into a bowl. In a separate bowl, mix together the bananas, sugar, butter, eggs, vanilla extract, chocolate chips, and walnuts. Add the flour mixture and combine, folding gently.

3. Put the batter into the prepared loaf pan. Bake in the preheated oven for 40–50 minutes, or until golden and risen.

4. Remove from the oven and cool in the pan for 40 minutes before transferring to a wire rack. Slice and serve with unsalted butter.

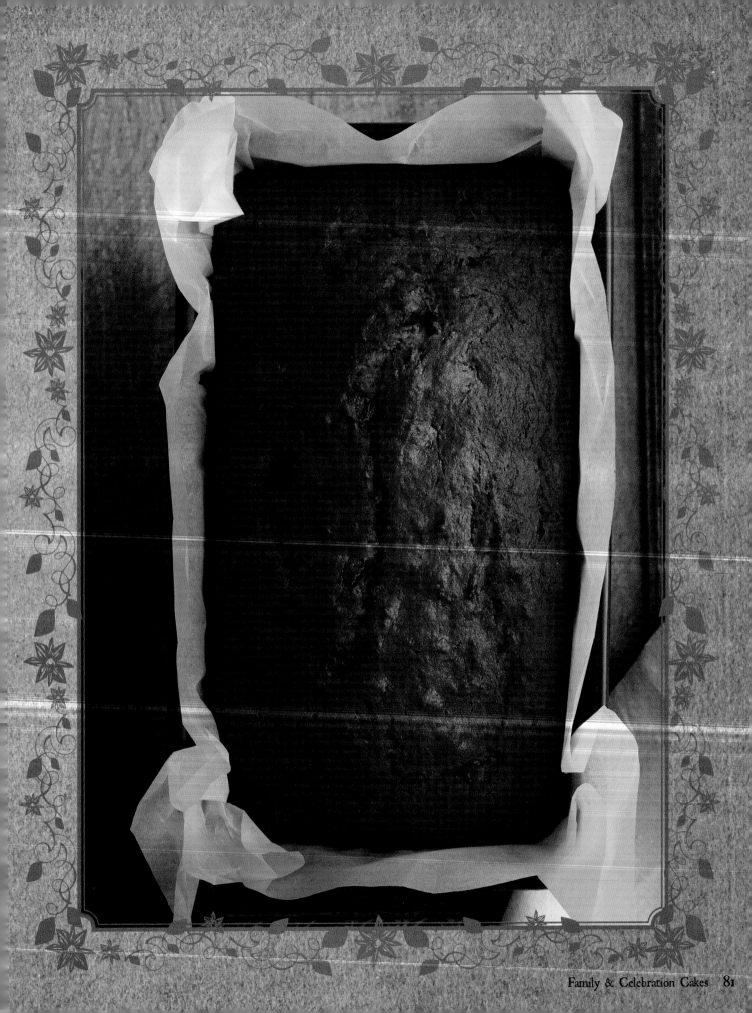

sticky fruit loaf

Prep Time: 15 minutes   Cook Time: 1 hr 15–45 minutes
Per loaf: 5,852 cal/284g fat/133g saturated fat/672g carbs/515g sugar/5.6g salt

makes 1 loaf

2½ cups golden raisin and raisin mixture

zest and juice of 1 lemon

2 sticks butter, plus extra for greasing

1 cup firmly packed dark brown sugar

½ teaspoon glycerin

5 eggs, beaten

2 cups gluten-free, wheat-free all-purpose flour

2 teaspoons allspice

3 tablespoons dark molasses

2 tablespoons whiskey

⅔ cup almond meal (ground almonds)

⅓ cup candied cherries

⅓ cup mixed seeds (such as sunflower and sesame)

1. Mix the dried fruits with the lemon zest and juice and ¼ cup warm water. Mix well and let soak for an hour or until the fruit is plump.

2. Preheat the oven to 300°F. Grease a 9-inch loaf pan and line with parchment paper.

3. Cream the butter, sugar, and glycerin in a large bowl. Add the eggs, one at a time, and stir in. Add the rest of the ingredients to the bowl and mix well.

4. Put the mixture into the pan and level it with a rubber spatula. Bake in the preheated oven for between 1 hour 15 minutes and 1 hour 45 minutes, or until a toothpick inserted in the center comes out clean.

5. Remove from the oven and cool in the pan for 40 minutes before transferring to a wire rack to cool completely. The loaf improves with age, so make it the day before you want to serve for a sticky, moist loaf. Store in an airtight container.

banana bread

Prep Time: 20 minutes   Cook Time: 50–60 minutes
Per loaf: 2,975 cal/59g fat/31g saturated fat/516g carbs/278g sugar/6.8g salt

makes 1 loaf

1 cup firmly packed dark brown sugar

2 eggs, beaten

1 cup mashed banana

3½ tablespoons butter, melted, plus extra for greasing

1 tablespoon dark molasses

½ cup buttermilk

3 cups gluten-free, wheat-free all-purpose flour

1 teaspoon gluten-free baking powder

1 teaspoon gluten-free baking soda

1 teaspoon allspice

unsalted butter, to serve

1. Preheat the oven to 350°F. Grease a 9-inch loaf pan and line with parchment paper.

2. Put the sugar, eggs, banana, melted butter, molasses, and buttermilk in a large bowl and mix well.

3. Sift together the flour, baking powder, baking soda, and allspice. Add to the bowl with the banana mixture and mix until combined.

4. Pour the batter into the prepared pan and bake in the preheated oven for 50–60 minutes, or until golden brown and firm to the touch.

5. Remove from the oven and cool in the pan for 40 minutes before transferring to a wire rack to cool completely. Serve warm or cold, sliced and spread with unsalted butter.

zucchini bread

Prep Time: 25 minutes   Cook Time: 1 hour
Per loaf: 2,430 cal/138g fat/18g saturated fat/235g carbs/116g sugar/2.9g salt

makes 2 loaves

butter, for greasing

3 cups gluten-free, wheat-free all-purpose flour

1 teaspoon gluten-free baking powder

2 teaspoons xanthan gum

1 teaspoon gluten-free baking soda

1 teaspoon allspice

2 teaspoons cinnamon

1 cup granulated sugar

3 eggs

1 cup vegetable oil

2 teaspoons vanilla extract

1 cup chopped walnuts

2 cups shredded zucchini

1. Preheat the oven to 325°F. Grease two 8½-inch loaf pans and line with parchment paper.

2. Sift together the flour, baking powder, xanthan gum, baking soda, and spices into a large bowl.

3. In a separate bowl, beat the sugar, eggs, vegetable oil, and vanilla extract until a creamy consistency forms. Add the flour mixture, walnuts, and zucchini to the bowl and fold in to make a smooth batter.

4. Divide the batter between the two pans and bake in the preheated oven for 55–60 minutes, until firm to the touch.

5. Let cool in the pans for about 20 minutes before transferring to a wire rack to cool. Let the bread rest on the rack for at least 30 minutes before serving.

angel food cake

Prep Time: 15 minutes   Cook Time: 45 minutes
Per cake: 2,643 cal/7g fat/3g saturated fat/579g carbs/407g sugar/3.9g salt

makes 1 cake

butter, for greasing

10 egg whites

⅓ cup white rice flour

½ cup tapioca flour

½ cup gluten-free cornstarch

½ cup potato flour

1½ cups granulated sugar

1½ teaspoons gluten-free cream of tartar

½ teaspoon vanilla extract

½ teaspoon salt

confectioners' sugar, to decorate

to serve

1 (1-pound) package frozen berries (optional)

½ cup granulated sugar (optional)

1. Preheat the oven to 350°F. Grease an 8-inch cake pan and line with parchment paper.

2. Let the egg whites sit for about 30 minutes at room temperature in a large bowl. In a separate bowl, sift in the white rice flour, tapioca flour, cornstarch, potato flour, and 1 cup of the sugar.

3. Using a food processor or mixer, mix the egg whites with the cream of tartar, vanilla extract, and salt until soft peaks form. Gradually add the remaining ½ cup of sugar until stiff peaks develop. Add the flour mixture and fold in.

4. Spoon the batter into the prepared pan and bake in the preheated oven for about 45 minutes, until firm to touch and a toothpick inserted in the center comes out clean.

5. Remove from the oven and, leaving the cake in the pan, turn upside down to cool on a wire rack. Poach the berries, if using, with the sugar gently until soft. Let cool completely. When the cake is cool, remove from the pan and decorate with confectioners' sugar and the drained mixed fruit, if desired.

black forest cake

Prep Time: 30 minutes   Cook Time: 20–25 minutes
Per cake: 8,498 cal/635g fat/345g saturated fat/637g carbs/503g sugar/7.1g salt

makes 1 cake

1 cup granulated sugar

1 stick butter,
plus extra for greasing

1 teaspoon glycerin

3 ounces gluten-free
semisweet dark chocolate,
broken into pieces

4 eggs

1 cup almond meal
(ground almonds)

1 cup gluten-free, wheat-free
all-purpose flour

1/4 cup gluten-free cornstarch

2 1/2 teaspoons gluten-free
baking powder

topping & filling

1 (15-ounce) can black
cherries, in syrup

2 tablespoons kirsch

1/3 cup black cherry preserves

3 cups heavy cream,
whipped

5 ounces gluten-free
semisweet dark chocolate,
grated, to decorate

fresh cherries, to decorate

1. Preheat the oven to 350°F. Grease two 8-inch cake pans and line with parchment paper.

2. Beat together the sugar, butter, and glycerin in a large bowl. Melt the chocolate in a heatproof bowl set over a saucepan of simmering water and let cool slightly. Beat the eggs, one at a time, into the sugar-and-butter mixture, adding the almonds with the final egg. Fold in the melted chocolate. Sift in the flour, cornstarch, and baking powder, then fold together gently.

3. Divide the batter between the two prepared pans and bake in the preheated oven for 20–25 minutes, until firm to the touch.

4. Remove from the oven and cool in the pans for 40 minutes. Drain the cherries reserving 1/2 cup of the syrup. Mix the kirsch with the cherry syrup and pour over the cakes.

5. When the cakes are cool, transfer them to a wire rack. Sandwich the cakes together with the preserves, the canned cherries, and half the cream. Spread the remaining cream on the top and sides of the cakes and decorate with grated chocolate and fresh cherries.

chocolate & raspberry cake

Prep Time: 30 minutes   Cook Time: 40 minutes
Per cake: 6,953 cal/514g fat/315g saturated fat/545g carbs/420g sugar/12.3g salt

makes 1 cake

1 cup gluten-free unsweetened cocoa powder, plus extra for dusting

1½ sticks butter, plus extra for greasing

1 cup full-bodied brewed coffee

1 cup granulated sugar

1 cup gluten-free, wheat-free all-purpose flour

1 teaspoon gluten-free baking powder

1 teaspoon gluten-free baking soda

¼ teaspoon xanthan gum

pinch of salt

2 eggs, beaten

½ cup whole-fat plain yogurt

1 tablespoon raspberry liqueur

1 teaspoon vanilla extract

frosting

1 cup granulated sugar

2½ cups heavy cream

2 pints raspberries, washed, to decorate

1. Preheat the oven to 350°F. Grease two 9-inch springform cake pans and line with parchment paper.

2. Put the cocoa powder, butter, and the coffee into a saucepan and simmer on low heat until the butter has melted. Remove from the heat, mix in the sugar, and set aside to cool slightly.

3. In a large bowl, mix together the flour, baking powder, baking soda, xanthan gum, and salt. Add the flour mixture to the cocoa mixture in the pan and stir in until combined. Add the eggs, one at time, and mix well. Add the yogurt, raspberry liqueur, and vanilla extract and stir well.

4. Divide the batter between the prepared pans and bake for 40 minutes, or until a toothpick inserted into the center comes out clean.

5. Remove from the oven and let the cakes cool in the pans for 20 minutes, then transfer them to a wire rack to finish cooling.

6. To make the frosting, whip together the sugar and cream in a large bowl. Use half the whipped cream and half the raspberries to sandwich the cakes together, then spread the remaining half of the cream on top of the cake and decorate with the remaining raspberries. Dust the top of the cake with cocoa powder.

strawberry shortcakes

Prep Time: 30 minutes   Cook Time: 20–25 minutes
Per shortcake: 482 cal/26g fat/16g saturated fat/59g carbs/26g sugar/0.5g salt

makes 8

⅔ cup tapioca flour

¾ cup brown rice flour

1 tablespoon gluten-free baking powder

⅔ cup gluten-free cornstarch

½ teaspoon xanthan gum

¼ teaspoon gluten-free baking soda

2 tablespoons almond meal (ground almonds)

5 tablespoons butter, plus extra for greasing

⅔ cup granulated sugar

¾ cup milk

strawberry filling

2 pints strawberries

2 tablespoons granulated sugar

1 cup heavy cream

confectioners' sugar, for dusting

1. Preheat the oven to 400°F. Grease a baking sheet and line with parchment paper.

2. Sift the tapioca flour, rice flour, baking powder, cornstarch, xanthan gum, baking soda, and almond meal into a bowl.

3. In a separate bowl, beat together the butter and sugar until it is fluffy. Add the flour mixture and fold in gently. Gradually add enough of the milk to the dry ingredients to form a soft dough.

4. Roll out the dough to a thickness of 1 inch. Use a 2¾-inch fluted round cutter to cut out circles of dough and place well apart on the baking sheet. Brush the tops with the remaining milk.

5. Bake in the preheated oven for 20–25 minutes, or until risen and golden. Remove from the oven and carefully transfer onto a wire rack to cool.

6. To make the filling, coarsely chop the strawberries. Place one-third in a blender, add the sugar, and process until smooth. Whip the cream, add half the remaining strawberries and the strawberry puree, and stir gently to swirl the mixture lightly. Halve the cooled shortcakes and spread the strawberry cream over the bottom halves. Sprinkle the remaining chopped strawberries on top. Place on the tops of the shortcakes and dust with confectioners' sugar. Serve immediately.

drambuie christmas cake

Prep Time: 40 minutes plus marinating   Cook Time: 2½–3 hours
Per cake: 15567 cal/433g fat/156g saturated fat/2,827g carbs/2,462g sugar/7.6g salt

makes 1 cake

¼ cup orange marmalade

½ cup chopped dried figs

⅔ cup chopped dates

1⅓ cups raisins

3½ cups golden raisins

½ cup chopped candied cherries

1½ cups chopped dried apricots

⅔ cup Drambuie, plus extra for drizzling

¾ cup firmly packed dark brown sugar

2 sticks butter, plus extra for greasing

4 extra-large eggs, beaten

2⅓ cups gluten-free, wheat-free all-purpose flour, sifted

1½ teaspoons allspice

⅔ cup blanched almonds, chopped

to decorate

3 tablespoons apricot preserves

2¼ pounds gluten-free marzipan

confectioners' sugar, for dusting

2¼ pounds gluten-free ready-to-use fondant

gluten-free silver balls

1. Mix the marmalade, all the fruit, and the Drambuie in a bowl, cover with plastic wrap, and let marinate over night.

2. Preheat the oven to 300°F. Grease an 8-inch square cake pan and line with parchment paper, extending the paper about 2–2½ inches above the pan.

3. Beat together the sugar and butter in a bowl by hand, or in a food processor, until fluffy. Add the eggs slowly, one at a time. Then add the marinated fruit mixture, the flour, allspice, and almonds and stir well.

4. Put the batter in the prepared pan, smooth the surface level, and bake in the preheated oven for about 2½–3 hours until a toothpick inserted into the center comes out clean.

5. Remove the cake from the pan and let cool. Remove the paper from the cake, then use a clean toothpick to pierce the surface of the cake and drizzle with Drambuie. Wrap in wax paper and aluminum foil and store in a cool place for three to four weeks.

6. To decorate, gently heat the preserves until runny, then push through a nylon strainer. Place the cake on a cake board. Brush the preserves over the top and sides of the cake. Roll out half the marzipan on a work surface dusted with confectioners' sugar and cut out a square large enough for the top of the cake. Roll out the remainder and use to cover the sides of the cake, trimming it to fit. Let dry for at least 24 hours.

7. Roll out the fondant on a work surface dusted with confectioners' sugar to a square large enough to cover the top and sides of the cake. Trim the edges, then smooth the surface. Use a star cutter to press into the fondant to create a shape and decorate with silver balls as desired.

lemon zest birthday cake

Prep Time: 25 minutes   Cook Time: 35–40 minutes
Per cake: 4,405 cal/202g fat/117g saturated fat/637g carbs/460g sugar/8.4g salt

makes 1 cake

2 sticks butter, plus extra for greasing

1 cup granulated sugar

4 eggs, beaten

1⅔ cups gluten-free, wheat-free self-rising flour

2 teaspoons gluten-free baking powder

1 teaspoon xanthan gum

juice and zest of 1 lemon

1⅔ cups raspberries, to decorate

lemon icing

2 cups gluten-free confectioners' sugar

juice and zest of 1 lemon

1. Preheat the oven to 350°F. Grease an 8-inch round springform cake pan and line with parchment paper.

2. Cream together the butter and sugar in a large bowl until fluffy. Slowly add the eggs, one at a time, and stir well. Sift in the flour, baking powder, and xanthan gum, then add the lemon juice and lemon zest and fold into the mixture.

3. Transfer the batter to the prepared pan, smooth out the top, and bake in the preheated oven for 35–40 minutes.

4. Remove the cake from the oven and let cool in the pan for 45 minutes before transferring it to a wire rack.

5. To make the icing, mix together the confectioners' sugar, lemon juice, and lemon zest in a large bowl. Drizzle the lemon icing over the cake and decorate with the raspberries to serve.

pumpkin & walnut cake

Prep Time: 20 minutes   Cook Time: 40–45 minutes
Per cake: 3,639 cal/240g fat/108g saturated fat/360g carbs/337g sugar/4.3g salt

makes 1 cake

1½ sticks butter, plus extra
for greasing

¾ cup firmly packed light
brown sugar

3 eggs, beaten

1 (15-ounce) can pumpkin
puree

1 teaspoon gluten-free
baking soda

3 tablespoons milk

4⅓ cups gluten-free, wheat-
free self-rising flour

1 teaspoon xanthan gum

½ teaspoon gluten-free
baking powder

¾ cup chopped walnuts

icing

1¼ cups confectioners' sugar

pulp and juice of
2 passion fruits

2 teaspoons lime zest

1. Preheat the oven to 350°F. Grease an 8-inch round springform cake pan and line with parchment paper.

2. Cream together the butter and sugar in a large bowl until fluffy. Stir in the eggs, slowly, one at a time, then stir in the pumpkin.

3. Add the baking soda to the milk and then add to the pumpkin mixture.

4. In a separate bowl, sift together the flour, xanthan gum, and baking powder and then fold the mixture into the pumpkin mixture with the walnuts.

5. Spoon the batter into the prepared cake pan and bake in the preheated oven for 40–45 minutes, until a toothpick inserted into the center comes out clean.

6. Remove from the oven and let cool in the pan for 10 minutes before transferring to a wire rack to cool completely.

7. To make the icing, sift the confectioners' sugar into a bowl and then add the passion fruit pulp and the lime zest. Stir well and pour over the cooled cake.

Chapter 4
Desserts & Pies

pear & apple oat crisp

Prep Time: 20 minutes   Cook Time: 30–35 minutes
Per serving: 275 cal/13g fat/7g saturated fat/34g carbs/27g sugar/2g salt

serves 8

filling

3 Pippin apples, peeled, cored, and sliced

3 Bosc pears, peeled, cored, and sliced

1 tablespoon apple juice

1/2 teaspoon gluten-free cornstarch

1/2 teaspoon cinnamon

2 tablespoons honey

2 cloves

light cream, to serve

oat crisp

1/2 cup gluten-free, wheat-free all-purpose flour

1/2 cup firmly packed light brown sugar

3 tablespoons chopped walnuts

2/3 cup gluten-free rolled oats

1 stick butter, plus extra for greasing

1. Preheat the oven to 325°F. Grease a 9-inch pie plate.

2. Put the apples, pears, apple juice, cornstarch, cinnamon, honey, and cloves in a bowl and stir well.

3. To make the crisp, mix the flour, sugar, walnuts, oats, and butter in a large bowl, rubbing together the ingredients with your fingertips.

4. Spread a small layer of crisp mixture over the bottom of the pie plate. Arrange the apple-and-pear mixture on top and sprinkle over the remaining crisp mixture.

5. Bake in the preheated oven for 30–35 minutes, until golden brown and crisp on top. Serve with fresh cream.

rhubarb & blackberry crisp

Prep Time: 25 minutes   Cook Time: 50–55 minutes
Per serving: 423 cal/16.5g fat/9g saturated fat/68g carbs/40g sugar/0.3g salt

serves 6

8–10 rhubarb stalks
(about 1¾ pounds),
cut into bite-size pieces

½ cup granulated sugar

2 cups blackberries

½ teaspoon vanilla extract

½ teaspoon ground ginger

ice cream or heavy cream,
to serve

crisp topping

1 stick butter, plus extra
for greasing

1⅔ cups gluten-free, wheat-
free all-purpose flour

½ cup raw brown sugar

2 tablespoons slivered
almonds

1. Preheat the oven to 350°F and grease a 9-inch ovenproof dish.

2. Place the rhubarb on a baking sheet, sprinkle with the granulated sugar, and roast in the oven for 12–15 minutes.

3. When cooked, put the rhubarb in the prepared dish with the blackberries, vanilla extract, and ginger.

4. For the topping, rub together the butter and flour with your fingertips until the mixture resembles fine bread crumbs. Add the raw sugar and almonds. Cover the rhubarb with the crisp topping and bake in the preheated oven for 35–40 minutes, until golden.

5. Serve with ice cream or heavy cream, as preferred.

almond & pear crunch cake

Prep Time: 30 minutes   Cook Time: 55–60 minutes
Per serving: 409 cal/25g fat/14g saturated fat/44g carbs/22g sugar/0.7g salt

serves 12

1½ sticks butter, plus extra for greasing

1 cup granulated sugar

3 extra-large eggs, beaten

½ teaspoon vanilla extract

1⅓ cups gluten-free, wheat-free all-purpose flour

2 teaspoons gluten-free baking powder

½ teaspoon cinnamon

⅓ cup almond meal (ground almonds)

1 (29-ounce) can pear halves, drained

whipped cream, to serve

crisp topping

1¼ cups gluten-free, wheat-free all-purpose flour

1 stick butter

¼ cup granulated sugar

1 handful of slivered almonds

1. Preheat the oven to 350°F. Grease an 8-inch cake pan and line with parchment paper.

2. Cream together the butter and sugar in a bowl until fluffy. Add the eggs slowly, one at a time, mixing well, then add the vanilla extract and stir.

3. Sift in the flour, baking powder, and cinnamon, and fold gently into the mixture. Add the almond meal and fold in.

4. Spoon the batter into the prepared pan and place the pear halves evenly on top, pushing them down a little.

5. To make the crisp topping, put the flour, butter, and sugar into a bowl and rub together, using your fingertips, to form the crisp. Sprinkle the crisp mixture over the top of the cake and sprinkle with the slivered almonds.

6. Bake on the middle shelf of the preheated oven for 55–60 minutes, until golden. Remove from the oven and cool in the pan. Serve with whipped cream.

upside-down banana & maple syrup cake

Prep Time: 30 minutes   Cook Time: 40–45 minutes
Per serving: 236 cal/13g fat/7g saturated fat/27g carbs/15g sugar/0.4g salt

serves 12

1½ sticks butter, plus extra for greasing

¼ cup firmly packed light brown sugar

¼ cup maple syrup, plus extra to serve

3–4 bananas, sliced lengthwise

1 cup granulated sugar

4 eggs, beaten

½ teaspoon vanilla extract

1¼ cups gluten-free, wheat-free self-rising flour

½ teaspoon xanthan gum

ice cream, to serve

1. Preheat the oven to 350°F. Grease a 9-inch round springform cake pan. Wrap a piece of aluminum foil around the outside of the pan to prevent the syrup from leaking.

2. Heat 4 tablespoons of the butter, the brown sugar, and maple syrup in a saucepan until the sugar melts and turns golden. Pour the mixture into the prepared pan and then arrange the sliced bananas, cut-side down, over the bottom.

3. Cream together the remaining butter and sugar in a bowl until fluffy. Add the eggs, one at a time, stirring well, and the vanilla extract. Sift in the flour and xanthan gum and fold gently into the batter.

4. Spoon the batter over the bananas and smooth with a rubber spatula.

5. Bake in the preheated oven for 40–45 minutes, until golden and the center springs back when lightly touched. Let cool in the pan on a wire rack.

6. Invert onto a serving plate, and serve with ice cream and maple syrup.

glazed brandy & date, bread & butter pudding

Prep Time: 30 minutes   Cook Time: 25–30 minutes
Per serving: 866 cal/51g fat/30g saturated fat/80g carbs/44g sugar/1.3g salt

serves 2

6 dates, diced

3 tablespoons brandy

1 tablespoon gluten-free sweet mincemeat

1 teaspoon granulated sugar

butter, for spreading and greasing

4–6 slices gluten-free white bread

2 teaspoons raw brown sugar

custard

½ cup milk

½ cup heavy cream

1 vanilla bean

1 egg

2 tablespoons superfine sugar or granulated sugar

1. Soak the dates in the brandy for 6 hours, or let soak overnight. Then add the mincemeat and granulated sugar to the date-and-brandy mixture.

2. Preheat the oven to 325°F and grease two 1-cup ovenproof dishes.

3. Remove the crusts from the bread, butter the slices, and cut into triangles. Fit a layer into the bottom of each dish. Alternate the date mixture and slices of bread until the dish is full. Finish off with slices of bread, buttered side down, at the top.

4. To make the custard, put the milk, cream, and vanilla bean into a saucepan and bring to the boil. Remove from the heat. In a bowl, whisk together the egg and sugar and pour the heated milk mixture into it.

5. Remove the vanilla bean and gradually pour the custard over the bread and butter pudding until it is absorbed. Let stand for 15–20 minutes.

6. Place the dishes in a roasting pan and sprinkle with the raw sugar. Pour boiling water in the pan to come halfway up the outside of the dishes. Cover the pan loosely with aluminum foil and bake for 20 minutes. Remove the foil and bake for an additional 5–10 minutes, or until the top is golden. For an extra crunchy top, put the dishes under a hot broiler for a couple of minutes, until caramelized. Serve warm or cold.

oven-baked molten chocolate lava cakes

Prep Time: 15 minutes   Cook Time: 15–18 minutes
Per serving: 686 cal/43g fat/23g saturated fat/73g carbs/60g sugar/0.7g salt

serves 4

7 ounces gluten-free semisweet dark chocolate, broken into pieces

1 stick unsalted butter, plus extra for greasing

3 tablespoons gluten-free, wheat-free all-purpose flour, sifted

3 eggs, beaten

½ cup granulated sugar

3 tablespoons almond meal (ground almonds)

1 teaspoon gluten-free baking powder

½ teaspoon vanilla extract

½ teaspoon glycerin

gluten-free unsweetened cocoa powder, for dusting

whipped cream, to serve

1. Preheat the oven to 400°F.

2. Place the chocolate and butter in a heatproof bowl and set over a saucepan of simmering water. Stir the mixture until it is just melted and then remove it from the heat.

3. Place the flour, eggs, sugar, almond meal, baking powder, vanilla extract, and glycerin in a bowl and mix until combined. Slowly stir in the chocolate mixture.

4. Grease four ¾-cup metal dariole (rum baba) molds. Divide the batter among the molds and place on a baking sheet. Bake the cakes in the preheated oven for 15–18 minutes.

5. Remove from the oven, gently run a knife around the edge of each cake, and invert onto a serving plate. Dust with cocoa and serve immediately with cream.

white chocolate & irish cream cheesecake

Prep Time: 30 minutes   Cook Time: 20 minutes, plus chilling time
Per serving: 794 cal/70g fat/42g saturated fat/36g carbs/19g sugar/1g salt

serves 12

cookie crust

12 ounces gluten-free, wheat-free graham crackers or cookies

1¼ sticks butter

filling

5 leaves gelatin

⅓ cup gluten-free white chocolate drops

2½ cups cream cheese

2½ cups heavy cream

½ cup granulated sugar

½ cup Irish cream liqueur

1 teaspoon vanilla extract

to decorate

2 tablespoons gluten-free white chocolate chips

gluten-free drinking chocolate mix, to dust

1. Crush the graham crackers using a food processor, or place them in a plastic bag and crush with a rolling pin.

2. Melt the butter in a small saucepan or in a nonmetallic bowl on low heat in the microwave. Add the cookie crumbs to the melted butter and mix well.

3. Press the crumb mixture into the bottom of an 8-inch round springform cake pan and chill in the refrigerator for about 30 minutes.

4. Place the gelatin leaves in a saucepan of cold water to soften.

5. Melt the white chocolate chips in a heatproof bowl set over a saucepan of simmering water.

6. Put the cream cheese, cream, sugar, Irish cream, and vanilla extract into a bowl and, using a whisk or electric mixer, whip slowly until thick and creamy. Mix in the melted chocolate.

7. Squeeze the water out of the gelatin leaves and place the leaves in a saucepan over low heat to melt. Add to the cream cheese mixture and stir in thoroughly and quickly before the gelatin sets.

8. Spoon the cream cheese mixture into the crust and smooth the top with a spatula. Refrigerate for 2–3 hours, until set.

9. To decorate, melt the white chocolate drops in a heatproof bowl set over a saucepan of simmering water. Spoon the chocolate into a pastry bag with a small tip and drizzle it over the top of the cheesecake. Dust the edge with drinking chocolate mix.

mini cherry pies

Prep Time: 30–35 minutes   Cook Time: 35–40 minutes
Per serving: 380 cal/10g fat/6g saturated fat/71g carbs/36g sugar/0.6g salt

makes 12

pastry dough

3⅔ cups gluten-free, wheat-free self-rising flour, plus extra for dusting

½ teaspoon xanthan gum

⅓ cup confectioners' sugar

1 stick butter, plus extra for greasing

½ cup milk, plus extra for glazing

1 egg, beaten

filling

4½ cups pitted fresh cherries or 2⅓ cups frozen cherries, thawed

1½ cups granulated sugar, plus extra for sprinkling

2 tablespoons gluten-free, wheat-free all-purpose flour

3 tablespoons gluten-free cornstarch

juice and zest of 1 lemon

1. Preheat the oven to 375°F. Grease a 12-cup muffin pan.

2. To make the pastry dough, sift the flour, xanthan gum, and confectioners' sugar into a large bowl. Rub in the butter using your fingertips until the mixture resembles fine bread crumbs, then add the milk and egg (reserving some of the egg for glazing), and combine to make the dough. Wrap the dough in plastic wrap and chill in the refrigerator for 30 minutes.

3. On a floured surface, roll out the dough to ⅛ inch thick and, using a 3½-inch round cookie cutter, cut out 12 circles to fit the prepared muffin cups. Press the dough circles into shape in the muffin cups.

4. In a bowl, combine the cherries, sugar, flour, cornstarch, and the juice and zest of the lemon. Divide the cherry mixture among the pastry shells. Roll out the remaining dough and cut into ½-inch-wide strips and use to make a crisscross lattice on top of the cherry filling, securing it at the edges with beaten egg.

5. Brush each pie with milk and sprinkle a little sugar on top. Bake in the preheated oven for 35–40 minutes, until golden brown on top. Remove from the oven and let cool in the muffin pan for at least 1 hour before serving.

strawberry & vanilla cheesecake

Prep Time: 30 minutes   Cook Time: 45–55 minutes plus chilling
Per serving: 706 cal/62g fat/38g saturated fat/33g carbs/15g sugar/1.3g salt

serves 12

cookie crust

10½ ounces gluten-free, wheat-free graham crackers or cookies

1¾ sticks butter, melted, plus extra for greasing

filling

4 cups cream cheese

½ cup granulated sugar

3 tablespoons gluten-free cornstarch

3 eggs

½ cup heavy cream

1¼ pints strawberries, washed and hulled

½ teaspoon vanilla extract

zest of 1 lemon

1. Preheat the oven to 400°F. Grease a 9-inch round springform cake pan and line the sides and bottom with parchment paper.

2. Crush the crackers using a food processor or place them in a plastic bag and crush them with a rolling pin.

3. Mix together the butter and cracker crumbs, press into the bottom of the pan, and bake in the preheated oven for 5 minutes. Remove from the oven and let cool.

4. Beat together the cream cheese, sugar, and cornstarch until light and creamy in consistency. Slowly add the eggs to the mixture and beat well, then slowly add the heavy cream to the mixture and beat until creamy.

5. Chop half the strawberries and add to the mixture with the vanilla extract and lemon zest.

6. Pour the mixture onto the crust and bake in the preheated oven for 45–55 minutes, or until the top is pale golden and the center set. Turn off the oven, leave the door ajar, and let stand until the cheesecake is cold—this prevents it from sinking. Chill in the refrigerator for at least 2 hours before serving. Release from the pan and decorate with the remaining fresh strawberries before serving.

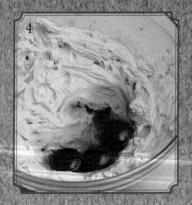

key lime pie

Prep Time: 30 minutes   Cook Time: 30 minutes plus chilling
Per serving: 580 cal/41g fat/23g saturated fat/50g carbs/32g sugar/0.8g salt

serves 10

cookie crust

10½ ounces gluten-free, wheat-free graham crackers or cookies

¼ cup granulated sugar

1¼ sticks butter, melted, plus extra for greasing

filling

4 egg yolks

1 (14-ounce) can condensed milk

juice of 6 limes (1 cup in total)

finely grated zest of 4 limes

1¼ cups heavy cream, to decorate

1. Preheat the oven to 350°F. Grease a 9-inch pie plate with melted butter.

2. Crush the graham crackers using a food processor or place them in a plastic bag and crush with a rolling pin. Mix together the sugar, crushed crackers, and melted butter in a large bowl.

3. Spread the crumb mixture over the bottom of the pie plate and up the sides, pressing firmly to pack it tight. Bake in the preheated oven for 10 minutes, then let cool.

4. To make the filling, whisk the egg yolks in a bowl and slowly add the condensed milk until creamy. Add the lime juice and zest, reserving some for decoration, and whip, using a whisk.

5. Pour the mixture into the pie plate and bake in the preheated oven for 20 minutes, or until the filling is firm with a slight wobble in the middle. Remove from the oven and let cool, then chill in the refrigerator for 3 hours.

6. When ready to serve, whip the heavy cream until it forms soft peaks, arrange small dollops of cream around the edge of the pie, and decorate with the reserved lime zest.

pumpkin pie

Prep Time: 30 minutes   Cook Time: 30–35 minutes
Per serving: 316 cal/22g fat/13g saturated fat/26g carbs/10.5g sugar/0.3g salt

serves 12

pastry dough

1⅔ cups gluten-free, wheat-free all-purpose flour, sifted, plus extra for dusting

2½ tablespoons rice flour

2 tablespoons confectioners' sugar

½ teaspoon xanthan gum

¼ teaspoon of salt

1 stick butter, plus extra for greasing

1 egg, beaten

2 tablespoons cold water

filling

2 eggs plus 1 egg yolk

1¼ cups heavy cream

⅓ cup firmly packed light brown sugar

1 tablespoon maple syrup

1¼ teaspoons cinnamon

½ teaspoon ground cloves

½ teaspoon ginger

1 cup canned pumpkin puree

vanilla cream, to serve

1. Preheat the oven to 350°F. Grease a 1½-inch deep, 9-inch fluted loose-bottom tart pan.

2. To make the pastry dough, place the flours, confectioners' sugar, xanthan gum, and salt in a mixing bowl. Add the butter and rub in with your fingertips until it resembles fine bread crumbs.

3. Make a well in the center of the mixture and add the egg and a little water. Using your hands, mix in the dry ingredients to form a dough. Invert the dough onto a floured surface and knead well. Wrap it in plastic wrap and chill in the refrigerator for 20–30 minutes.

4. Roll out to a thickness of ⅛ inch and use it to line the greased tart pan. Line the pastry shell with parchment paper and pie weights or dried beans and bake in the preheated oven for 12 minutes, until golden. Remove the parchment paper and weights.

5. Whisk the eggs and yolk in a bowl. Put the cream, brown sugar, maple syrup, and spices in a saucepan and heat gently, being careful not to let them boil. Cool slightly, then add to the egg mixture and whisk together. Add the pumpkin puree and mix well.

6. Pour the mixture into the pastry shell and bake in the preheated oven for 30–35 minutes, until firm to the touch. Remove from the oven and serve warm with vanilla cream.

pecan pie

Prep Time: 1–1½ hours   Cook Time: 50–55 minutes
Per serving: 363 cal/24g fat/8.5g saturated fat/33g carbs/17g sugar/0.4g salt

serves 12

pastry dough

1⅔ cups gluten-free, wheat-free all-purpose flour, sifted

2½ tablespoons rice flour

2 tablespoons confectioners' sugar

½ teaspoon xanthan gum

¼ teaspoon of salt

1 stick butter, plus extra for greasing

1 egg, beaten

2 tablespoons cold water

filling

½ cup granulated sugar

3 extra-large eggs

⅓ cup light corn syrup

2 tablespoons bourbon

3 tablespoons butter, melted

½ teaspoon vanilla extract

1¾ cups pecan halves

vanilla ice cream, to serve

1. Preheat the oven to 350°F. Grease a 1½-inch deep, 9-inch fluted loose-bottom tart pan.

2. Place the flours, confectioners' sugar, xanthan gum, and salt in a mixing bowl. Add the butter and rub in using your fingertips until it resembles fine bread crumbs.

3. Make a well in the center of the mixture and add the egg and the water. Using your hands, mix in the dry ingredients to form a dough. Invert it onto a floured surface and knead well. Wrap it in plastic wrap and chill in the refrigerator for 20–30 minutes.

4. Roll out the dough to a thickness of ⅛ inch and use it to line the greased tart pan. Line the prepared pastry shell with parchment paper and pie weights or dried beans and bake in the preheated oven for 12 minutes, until golden. Remove the parchment paper and weights.

5. To make the filling, whisk the sugar and the eggs in a bowl. Slowly stir in the light corn syrup, bourbon, butter, and vanilla extract. Sprinkle the pecans over the cooked pastry bottom. Pour the filling over the nuts and return to the oven. Bake for 35–40 minutes, until just golden.

6. Remove from the oven. Serve warm or cold with vanilla ice cream.

strawberry & vanilla cream puffs

Prep Time: 30 minutes   Cook Time: 25 minutes
Per serving: 953 cal/78g fat/47g saturated fat/57g carbs/41g sugar/0.4g salt

serves 7

choux pastry dough

1 stick butter

1 teaspoon superfine sugar
or granulated sugar

½ cup water

1 cup gluten-free, wheat-free
all-purpose flour, sifted

4 eggs

cream filling

2½ cups heavy cream

1 teaspoon vanilla extract

1⅓ cups hulled and finely
diced strawberries

chocolate sauce

¼ cup granulated sugar

⅔ cup water

6 ounces gluten-free
semisweet dark chocolate,
broken into pieces

1 tablespoon butter

1. Preheat the oven to 400°F. Line a baking sheet with parchment paper.

2. To make the choux pastry dough, heat the butter and sugar in a saucepan with the water and bring to a boil. Add the flour and remove from the heat. Mix with a spatula until a dough ball forms. Let the mixture cool for 10–15 minutes.

3. When cool, beat in the eggs slowly until the dough is smooth and glossy. Spoon the dough into a pastry bag fitted with a ¾-inch plain tip and pipe about 35 small balls onto the baking sheet. Each ball should be about the size of a walnut. Using a wet finger, rub the top of each ball to get rid of any lumps or bumps.

4. Bake in the preheated oven for 15–20 minutes, until golden brown (if they are too pale, they will turn soggy). Remove from the oven and prick the bottom of each puff with the tip of a sharp knife to release the steam. Return to the baking sheet, with the hole facing upward, to dry out the center for 5–6 minutes.

5. To make the filling, whip the heavy cream with the vanilla extract. Add the diced strawberries and stir. Spoon the mixture into a pastry bag and pipe into the cooled puffs.

6. To make the chocolate sauce, heat the sugar and water in a small saucepan, stirring until dissolved. Bring to a boil, remove from the heat, add the chocolate pieces and butter, and stir until melted and smooth.

7. Arrange the puffs on serving dishes and pour over the chocolate sauce. Serve immediately.

oven-baked chocolate & pistachio tart

Prep Time: 30 minutes   Cook Time: 40–50 minutes plus chilling
Per serving: 480 cal/29g fat/15g saturated fat/47g carbs/30g sugar/0.7g salt

serves 12

pastry dough

1²⁄₃ cups gluten-free, wheat-free all-purpose flour

2½ tablespoons rice flour

2 tablespoons confectioners' sugar

½ teaspoon xanthan gum

¼ teaspoon salt

1 stick butter, plus extra for greasing

1 egg, beaten

2 tablespoons cold water

vanilla ice cream and strawberries, to serve

filling

5 ounces gluten-free semisweet dark chocolate, broken into pieces

1¼ sticks butter

⅓ cup gluten-free unsweetened cocoa powder

4 eggs

1 cup granulated sugar

3 tablespoons light corn syrup

¾ cup roasted pistachio nuts, chopped

1. Preheat the oven to 300°F. Grease a 1½-inch deep, 9-inch fluted loose-bottomed tart pan.

2. To make the pastry dough, sift the flours, confectioners' sugar, xanthan gum, and salt in a mixing bowl. Add the butter and rub in using your fingertips until the mixture resembles fine bread crumbs.

3. Make a well in the center of the mixture and add the egg and a little water. Using your hands, mix in the dry ingredients to form a dough. Invert it onto a floured surface and knead well. Wrap it in plastic wrap and chill in the refrigerator for 20–30 minutes.

4. Roll out the pastry dough to a thickness of ⅛ inch and use it to line the greased tart pan. Line the prepared pastry shell with parchment paper, fill with pie weights or dried beans, and bake in the preheated oven for 12 minutes, until golden. Remove the parchment paper and weights.

5. To make the filling, melt the chocolate, butter, and cocoa powder in a heatproof bowl set over a saucepan of simmering water, stirring continuously.

6. In a bowl, whisk together the eggs, sugar, and light corn syrup until light and creamy. Then add the chocolate mixture and pistachio nuts and mix well.

7. Fill the tart shell with the chocolate and pistachio mixture and bake in the preheated oven for 40–50 minutes. Remove from the oven and let cool for about 30–60 minutes. Serve with vanilla ice cream and strawberries.

lemon meringue pie

Prep Time: 30 minutes   Cook Time: 35 minutes
Per serving: 415 cal/19g fat/10g saturated fat/60g carbs/36g sugar/0.5g salt

serves 12

for the pastry dough

1²⁄₃ cups gluten-free, wheat-free all-purpose flour, sifted

2½ tablespoons rice flour

2 tablespoons confectioners' sugar

½ teaspoon xanthan gum

¼ teaspoon salt

1 stick butter

1 egg, beaten

2 tablespoons cold water

lemon filling

juice and zest of 4 lemons

½ cup superfine sugar

⅓ cup gluten-free cornstarch

6 egg yolks

1 stick butter

meringue

6 egg whites

1 teaspoon gluten-free cornstarch

½ teaspoon white wine vinegar

½ cup superfine sugar

1. Preheat the oven to 300°F. Grease a 1½-inch deep, 9-inch fluted loose-bottomed tart pan.

2. Sift the flours, confectioners' sugar, xanthan gum, and salt into a mixing bowl. Add the butter and rub in with your fingertips until it resembles fine bread crumbs. Make a well in the center of the mixture and add the egg and a little water. Using your hands, mix in the dry ingredients to form a dough. Turn out the dough onto a floured surface and knead well. Wrap it in plastic wrap and chill in the refrigerator for 20–30 minutes.

3. Roll the dough out to a thickness of ⅛ inch and use it to line the greased tart pan. Line the prepared pastry shell with parchment paper and pie weights or dried beans and bake in the preheated oven for 12 minutes, until golden. Remove the parchment paper and weights.

4. To make the filling, measure the lemon juice and make up to 1¼ cups with water. Transfer to a pan with the lemon zest and sugar and bring to a boil. Mix the cornstarch to a paste with a little water, add to the hot lemon mix and simmer, stirring continuously, for 1 minute, until the mixture has boiled and thickened. Remove from the heat and let cool for 5 minutes. Gradually add the egg yolks and butter, beating well between additions. Pour the mixture into the pastry shell and let stand until cold and set. Increase the oven temperature to 350°F.

5. To make the meringue, whisk the egg whites, cornstarch, and vinegar in a bowl until they form stiff peaks. Slowly add the sugar, whisking until the meringue is stiff and glossy.

6. Pipe or spoon the meringue on top of the lemon pie, making sure the meringue goes right to the edge. Bake in the preheated oven for 10–15 minutes, until golden brown. Remove from the oven and serve warm or cool.

3

4

6

old-fashioned apple pie

Prep Time: 1 hour 15 minutes   Cook Time: 35–40 minutes
Per serving: 464 cal/15g fat/9g saturated fat/80g carbs/36g sugar/0.8g salt

serves 8

pastry dough

3⅔ cups gluten-free, wheat-free self-rising flour, plus extra for dusting

½ teaspoon xanthan gum

⅓ cup confectioners' sugar

1 stick butter, plus extra for greasing

1 extra-large egg, beaten

½ cup milk, plus extra for glazing

ice cream, to serve

filling

7–8 Granny Smith apples, cored, peeled, and sliced

½ cup granulated sugar, plus extra for sprinkling

1 teaspoon gluten-free cornstarch

2 tablespoons water

1 teaspoon cinnamon

2 cloves

1. Preheat the oven to 350°F. Grease an 8–10-inch ovenproof pie plate.

2. To make the filling, put the sliced apple, sugar, cornstarch, water, cinnamon, and cloves into a saucepan and cook until the apple is just tender. Drain the apple mixture in a strainer and let cool.

3. To make the pastry dough, sift the flour, xanthan gum, and confectioners' sugar into a large bowl. Rub in the butter with your fingertips until the mixture resembles fine bread crumbs. Add the egg (reserving a little for glazing) together with the milk and combine to make the dough. Wrap in plastic wrap and chill in the refrigerator for 20 minutes.

4. On a floured surface, divide the dough in two and roll each piece out to form a large circle—one to line the pie plate and one to go on top of the pie. Line the pie plate with one of the pastry circles and add the apple filling.

5. Mix together a little milk and egg and brush the rim of the pastry with this. Add the second pastry circle as a lid and, using a fork, crimp the edges of the pastry all the way around. Pierce the pie in the middle a couple of times to let out steam during baking.

6. Brush the top of the pie with the milk-and-egg mixture and sprinkle with sugar. Bake in the preheated oven for 35–40 minutes, until golden.

7. Remove from the oven and sprinkle with a little more sugar and serve with ice cream.

Chapter 5
Breads & Savory Pastries

seven grain bread

Prep Time: 2 hours plus rising   Cook Time: 40–45 minutes
Per loaf: 2,628 cal/87g fat/12g saturated fat/383g carbs/31g sugar/1.7g salt

makes 1 loaf

butter, for greasing

½ cup amaranth flour

¾ cup brown rice flour

⅔ cup sorghum flour

½ cup gluten-free cornstarch

½ cup tapioca flour

4 teaspoons ground
chia seeds

1 cup ground flaxseed

2 teaspoons xanthan gum

2 teaspoons active dry yeast

1 teaspoon salt

3 eggs

1 tablespoon vegetable oil

2 tablespoons sugar

1 cup lukewarm water

1 tablespoon sunflower seeds

1. Grease an 8½-inch loaf pan.

2. Combine together the flours, chia seeds, flaxseed, xanthan gum, yeast, and salt in a bowl.

3. In a separate bowl, mix together the eggs, vegetable oil, sugar, and water until well combined. Add the dry ingredients to the egg mixture and mix well to form a soft dough.

4. Put the dough into the prepared pan, sprinkle with the sunflower seeds, and cover with a clean damp dish towel for an hour, until the dough rises. Preheat the oven to 350°F.

5. Remove the dish towel and bake the loaf in the preheated oven for 40–45 minutes, until golden brown.

oven-baked rolls

Prep Time: 30 minutes plus rising   Cook Time: 20–25 minutes
Per roll: 184 cal/4g fat/1g saturated fat/33g carbs/3g sugar/0.3g salt

makes 24

4 eggs

¼ cup vegetable oil

⅓ cup granulated sugar

1 tablespoon xanthan gum

¾ cup potato flour

3 cups white rice flour, plus extra for dusting

1¾ cups tapioca flour

¾ cup buckwheat flour

1 tablespoon active dry yeast

1 teaspoon salt

1¼ cups lukewarm milk

1. Preheat the oven to 375°F. Line one or two baking sheets with parchment paper.

2. Combine the eggs, vegetable oil, and sugar in a large bowl and mix well with an electric mixer.

3. Add the xanthan gum, potato flour, white rice flour, tapioca flour, buckwheat flour, yeast, and salt and combine well, gradually adding the lukewarm milk until a thick bread dough is formed.

4. Transfer the dough from the bowl to a floured surface and knead for 1–2 minutes. Divide and shape the dough into 24 balls, using extra flour, if necessary, to prevent the dough from sticking.

5. Place the rolls on the baking sheet, cover with a clean damp dish towel, and let them rise at room temperature for 45–60 minutes, until they have almost doubled in size.

6. Bake in the preheated oven for 20–25 minutes, until golden brown. Remove from the oven and cool on a wire rack.

mixed grain bread

Prep Time: 30 minutes plus rising   Cook Time: 30 minutes
Per loaf: 3,697 cal/179g fat/19g saturated fat/417g carbs/16g sugar/5.8g salt

makes 1 loaf

butter, for greasing

2½ teaspoons dry yeast

2 cups lukewarm water

1 tablespoon maple syrup

1⅓ cups gluten-free oat flour

1 cup rice flour

1 cup almond flour

1 cup buckwheat flour

2 tablespoons tapioca flour

½ cup quinoa flour

1 teaspoon xanthan gum

1 teaspoon salt

3 eggs, beaten

¼ cup sunflower oil

1 tablespoon gluten-free rolled oats

1. Grease and line a 9-inch loaf pan with parchment paper.

2. Mix the yeast with ½ cup of the warm water and add the maple syrup. Mix well and let stand at room temperature for 10–15 minutes, until frothy.

3. Mix all the flours, xanthan gum, and salt in a large bowl. Make a well in the middle of the mixture and add the yeast liquid.

4. Add the eggs and the sunflower oil and mix together, adding the remaining water a little at a time to form a firm dough. Invert onto a lightly floured surface and knead for about 5 minutes, until smooth and elastic.

5. Shape the loaf and place in the pan. Brush with a little water then sprinkle with the oats. Cover with a clean damp dish towel and let stand in a warm place until the loaf has risen and is twice its size.

6. Preheat the oven to 350°F. Bake in the preheated oven for 30 minutes, or until golden and crusty. Cool in the pan for 5 minutes, then invert onto a wire rack to cool completely.

caramelized onion, thyme & olive focaccia bread

Prep Time: 30 minutes plus rising   Cook Time: 30–35 minutes
Per loaf: 2,586 cal/88g fat/45g saturated fat/393g carbs/44g sugar/7.5g salt

makes 1 loaf

butter, for greasing

3½ cups gluten-free, wheat-free white bread flour

2 teaspoons dry yeast

2 teaspoons granulated sugar

1½ cups lukewarm milk

2 eggs, beaten

1 garlic clove, finely chopped

10–12 ripe black olives

kosher salt

cracked black pepper

grated Parmesan cheese, for sprinkling

caramelized onion

3½ tablespoons butter

2 small red onions, thinly sliced

4–5 sprigs thyme

1. To make the caramelized onion, melt the butter in a small skillet and sauté the onion and thyme gently until the onion is soft and caramelized. Remove from the heat and cool until required.

2. Grease a 10 x 14-inch baking sheet and line with parchment paper.

3. Sift the flour into a bowl. In a separate bowl or pitcher, mix the yeast, sugar, and lukewarm milk and let stand for 5–10 minutes at room temperature until frothy. Mix in the eggs and add the liquid mixture to the flour and mix well.

4. Transfer the dough to the prepared sheet, cover with a clean damp dish towel, and let stand for about 45 minutes, until it has doubled in size. Preheat the oven to 350°F.

5. Spread the caramelized onion over the top of the bread and sprinkle with the garlic, olives, salt, pepper, and Parmesan. Press the toppings lightly into the bread, using your fingers.

6. Bake in the preheated oven for 30–35 minutes, until golden and crusty. Remove from the oven and let cool on a wire rack. The bread can be served hot or cold.

tortilla wraps

Prep Time: 15–20 minutes plus standing   Cook Time: 5–6 minutes per wrap
Per tortilla: 160 cal/3g fat/0.5g saturated fat/31g carbs/0.6g sugar/trace salt

makes 10

2½ teaspoons dry yeast

1¾ cups lukewarm water

2 tablespoons sunflower oil

3¼ cups gluten-free, wheat-free all-purpose flour, plus extra for dusting

1½ teaspoons xanthan gum

2 tablespoons chopped cilantro (optional)

½ teaspoon crushed red pepper (optional)

salt and pepper

1. Mix the yeast, lukewarm water, and oil in a small bowl and let stand at room temperature for about 20 minutes, until frothy.

2. Sift the flour and xanthan gum into a large bowl and make a well in the center. Add the yeast liquid to the well slowly with the cilantro, crushed red pepper, if using, salt, and pepper. Mix well to form a sticky dough.

3. Invert onto a floured surface and knead well. Divide into 8–10 small balls.

4. Cut out an 8-inch circle of parchment paper and roll out each ball of dough under it, the thinner the better.

5. Place a nonstick skillet on medium heat. Add the tortillas to the skillet, one at a time, with the parchment paper underneath and cook for 2–3 minutes, until golden brown. Flip over, remove the paper, and cook the other side for 2–3 minutes, until golden brown. If the paper starts to scorch, cut a new circle.

6. Serve hot or cold with your favorite fillings. To store, stack each tortilla between parchment paper to prevent them from sticking and keep in an airtight container for up to one week or freeze for one to two months.

pizza crusts

Prep Time: 30–40 minutes   Cook Time: 25 minutes
Per crust: 353 cal/5.5g fat/1g saturated fat/65g carbs/5g sugar/1.5g salt

makes 4 crusts

1 cup lukewarm water

3 tablespoons instant dry milk

1 teaspoon sugar

1 tablespoon dry yeast

1 cup gluten-free, wheat-free bread flour, sifted, plus extra for dusting

1 cup rice flour

2 teaspoon gluten-free baking powder

1 teaspoon salt

½ teaspoon xanthan gum

1 egg

1 tablespoon sunflower oil

pizza sauce and toppings of your choice, to serve

1. Place the lukewarm water in a bowl and dissolve the dry milk, sugar, and yeast in it. Let stand at room temperature for about 5–10 minutes, until frothy.

2. In a large bowl, mix together the bread flour, rice flour, baking powder, salt, and xanthan gum.

3. In a separate bowl, whisk together the egg and sunflower oil and then add to the dry mixture. Pour in the yeast liquid and continue to mix until a soft dough forms.

4. On a floured surface, roll out the dough and divide into four equal ball. Cut out four circles of parchment paper 8 inches in diameter and roll out the dough to fit each circle. Cover the pizza crusts with a clean, damp dish towel for 10–15 minutes before baking. Preheat the oven to 400°F.

5. Place the pizza crusts, with the parchment paper, on a baking sheet and bake in the preheated oven for 10 minutes.

6. Remove from the oven, add your pizza sauce and favorite toppings, and return to the oven and bake for another 10–15 minutes.

pear, oat & blueberry breakfast loaf

Prep Time: 30 minutes   Cook Time: 55 minutes–1 hour
Per loaf: 2,982 cal/114g fat/61g saturated fat/471g carbs/287g sugar/6.9g salt

makes 1 loaf

1 cup granulated sugar

1 stick butter, plus extra for greasing

2 extra-large eggs, beaten

½ teaspoon vanilla extract

1 cup gluten-free, wheat-free all-purpose flour, sifted

1 teaspoon gluten-free baking powder

½ teaspoon gluten-free baking soda

¼ teaspoon xanthan gum

1 cup gluten-free, wheat-free oats, plus extra for sprinkling

pinch of salt

½ teaspoon ground cinnamon

3 bananas, mashed

¼ cup milk

2 cooked or canned pear halves, diced

½ cup blueberries

raw brown sugar, for sprinkling

1. Preheat the oven to 350°F. Grease a 9-inch loaf pan and line with parchment paper.

2. Cream the sugar and butter in a bowl. Add the eggs and vanilla extract slowly.

3. In a separate bowl, mix together the flour, baking powder, baking soda, xanthan gum, oats, salt, and cinnamon, then add the dry mixture to the egg mixture. Add the mashed banana and milk and mix well until combined.

4. Spoon half of the batter into the prepared loaf pan, then sprinkle with the diced pear and two-thirds of the blueberries. Spoon the remaining batter on top. Sprinkle with the remaining blueberries, the oats, and the raw sugar.

5. Bake in the preheated oven for 55 minutes–1 hour, or until a toothpick inserted in the center comes out clean. Remove from the oven and let cool in the pan.

deep-filled chicken & oyster mushroom pie

Prep Time: 30 minutes plus chilling   Cook Time: 30–40 minutes
Per serving: 641 cal/42g fat/25g saturated fat/39g carbs/4.5g sugar/1.1g salt

serves 6

pastry dough

1¾ cups gluten-free, wheat-free, all-purpose flour

½ cup grated Parmesan cheese

½ teaspoon xanthan gum

pinch of salt

1 stick butter

1 egg, beaten

filling

3½ tablespoons butter

1 small white onion, diced

4 cups chopped white button mushrooms

6 ounces oyster mushrooms, torn into strips

2 teaspoons crushed garlic

3 tablespoons gluten-free, wheat-free all-purpose flour

1½ cups milk

juice of 1 lime

⅔ cup crème fraîche or sour cream

2 teaspoons dried tarragon

3 cups freshly cooked chicken chunks

1 egg yolk, beaten

salt and pepper

1. Place the flour, Parmesan cheese, xanthan gum, and salt into a bowl. Add the butter and rub in with your fingertips until it resembles fine bread crumbs. Make a well in the center of the mixture and add the egg and a little water. Using your hands, mix in the dry ingredients to form a dough. Invert it onto a floured surface and knead well. Wrap it in plastic wrap and chill in the refrigerator for 20–30 minutes.

2. To make the filling, melt the butter in a small saucepan and sauté the onion and mushrooms gently until soft. Add the garlic and season with salt and pepper. Add the flour and cook for 2–3 minutes, mixing the flour through the mushroom mixture.

3. Remove the pan from the heat and slowly add the milk. When all the milk has been added, put the pan back on the heat and stir well, until the sauce bubbles and becomes smooth. Cook for 2–3 minutes on low heat and then set aside. Add the lime juice, crème fraîche, tarragon, and cooked chicken to the cooling mixture. Preheat the oven to 350°F. Grease a deep 9-inch pie plate.

4. Place a pie funnel in the center of the pie plate, then spoon in the filling around it. Roll out the dough and cut an oval slightly larger than the top of the pie. Slice the trimmings into ½-inch-wide strips and attach them to the rim of the pie plate, using a little water. Brush these edges with water, then lift the dough on top of the pie. Trim the edges, then seal and crimp the pastry. Make a cut so the top of the funnel sticks out of the pastry. Use any leftover dough to decorate the top of the pie. Brush the top of the pie with the beaten egg yolk and make a couple of slits in the top with a sharp knife to let the steam escape.

5. Bake in the preheated oven for 30–40 minutes, until the pastry is golden and flaky. Serve immediately. As an alternative, the pie could be topped with mashed potatoes instead of the pastry.

roasted tomato, asparagus & swiss cheese quiche

Prep Time: 30 minutes plus chilling　　Cook Time: 45–50 minutes
Per serving: 466 cal/37g fat/21g saturated fat/24g carbs/2g sugar/0.8g salt

serves 8

pastry dough

1¾ cups gluten-free, wheat-free all-purpose flour, plus extra for dusting

½ teaspoon xanthan gum

½ teaspoon salt

1 stick butter, plus extra for greasing

1 egg, beaten

¼ cup water

filling

8–10 asparagus stems

3 eggs plus 1 egg yolk

1 cup heavy cream

1 shallot, diced

1 cup shredded Swiss cheese or Gruyère cheese

1 tablespoon snipped chives

1 tablespoon flat-leaf parsley, chopped

12–14 cherry tomatoes

salt and pepper

1. Grease a deep, 9-inch, fluted loose-bottomed tart pan.

2. To make the pastry dough, place the flour, xanthan gum, and salt into a bowl. Add the butter and rub in with your fingertips until it resembles fine bread crumbs.

3. Make a well in the center of the mixture and add the egg and a little water. Using your hands, mix in the dry ingredients to form a dough. Invert it onto a floured surface and knead well. Wrap it in plastic wrap and chill in the refrigerator for 20–30 minutes.

4. Roll out the dough and use it to line the prepared tart pan. Place in the freezer for 20 minutes. Preheat the oven to 350°F.

5. Remove the dough from the freezer, line with parchment paper, fill with pie weights or dried beans, and bake in the preheated oven for 10 minutes. Remove the parchment paper and weights and let the pastry cool slightly before adding the filling.

6. To make the filling, cut the asparagus stems in half. Cook in boiling salted water for 3 minutes, or until just tender. Drain, rinse in cold water, and drain again. Beat together the eggs, egg yolk, and cream with salt and pepper. Sprinkle the shallot, half the cheese, and half the chives and parsley over the pastry bottom. Top with the blanched asparagus, cherry tomatoes, and remaining cheese and herbs. Pour the eggs mixture over the vegetables.

7. Return the quiche to the oven, reduce the temperature to 325°F, and bake for 25–30 minutes, or until the top is golden and the filling set. Serve warm or cool.

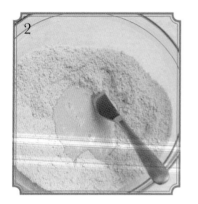

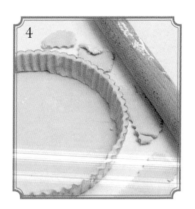

individual chicken & ham pot pies

Prep Time: 30 minutes plus chilling   Cook Time: 2 hours 15 minutes
Per pie: 1,011 cal/63g fat/37g saturated fat/56g carbs/3g sugar/2.7g salt

serves 6

pastry dough

3⅔ cups gluten-free, wheat-free all-purpose flour, plus extra for dusting

½ cup grated Parmesan cheese

½ teaspoon xanthan gum

½ teaspoon salt

2 sticks butter, plus extra for greasing

2 eggs, beaten

filling

4-pound chicken

1 leek, chopped

1 garlic clove

2 thyme sprigs

1½ cups heavy cream

¼ cup gluten-free, wheat-free all-purpose flour

4 tablespoons butter, softened

6 cups white button mushrooms, halved

1 pound cooked ham, chopped into large chunks

1⅓ cups corn kernels

2 scallions, chopped

3 tablespoons chopped chives

salt and pepper

greens and mashed potatoes, to serve

1. Place the chicken in a large pot with the leek, garlic, and thyme and cover with water. Bring to a boil, reduce the heat, cover, and simmer for 1 hour–1 hour 20 minutes, until a meat thermometer inserted into the thickest part of the meat—in the inner thigh area near the breast—without touching the bone, has a reading of 180°F. Or cook until the chicken is tender and the juices run clear when the tip of a sharp knife is inserted into the thickest part of the meat. Remove the chicken from the pot and cool. Simmer the remaining stock down to 3½ cups.

2. Preheat the oven to 350°F. Grease six 1¾-cup pie plates.

3. To make the pastry dough, place the flour, Parmesan cheese, xanthan gum, and salt into a bowl. Add the butter and rub in with your fingertips until it resembles fine bread crumbs. Make a well in the center of the mixture and add the eggs (reserving some of the egg for glazing) and a little water. Using your hands, mix in the dry ingredients to form a dough. Invert it onto a floured surface and knead well. Wrap the dough in plastic wrap and chill in the refrigerator for 20–30 minutes.

4. To make the sauce, add the cream to the reserved chicken stock and bring to a boil. Mix together the flour and butter and then gradually add it to the boiling stock, whisking well until the sauce thickens. Remove from the heat and let cool. Chop the cooked chicken, add to the sauce with the mushrooms, ham, corn, onions, and chives, and season with salt and pepper. Divide the mixture among the prepared pie plates.

5. Roll out the dough and cut out six ovals slightly larger than the pie plates. Slice the trimmings into ½-inch-wide strips and attach them to the rims of the plates, using a little water. Brush these edges with water, then lift the pastry tops onto the pies. Trim the edges, then seal and crimp the pastry and brush with a little beaten egg. Make a couple of slits in the top with a sharp knife to let the steam escape.

6. Bake in the preheated oven for 30–40 minutes, until golden. Remove from the oven and serve with greens and mashed potato.